C000006231

Mysteries of th

By
Kenneth Edward Barnes

Copyright © 2015 Kenneth Edward Barnes. All rights reserved.

This book is dedicated to the Word of God, for without the Word I would have no book, no life or no hope. "The Word became flesh and dwelt among us", John 1:14.

I wish to thank my wife, Lilly, for the many times she has proof read my work, her suggestions, editing and comments. I would also like to thank my brother, Messianic Rabbi Tom, for his help with Greek/Hebrew Scriptures. If you would like to receive my brother's Bible teachings, go to his web site to be put on the list. It is free and it may help you understand many Scriptures that have been mistranslated or are little understood.

Contents

Introduction

In this book of 64,000 words, I will try to reveal some startling verses of Scripture that will shed light on some mysteries that have been hidden for centuries. Why am I writing this book and why am I qualified to write it? The Bible says in 2 Timothy 2:15, "Study to show yourself approved unto God, a workman that needs not to be ashamed, rightly dividing the word of truth."

I am in my latter years and none of us knows how many days we have left on this earth. I wanted to write this before I leave this life so others might come to know and understand what I have searched for my entire life. The Lord said, "Lay up your treasures in heaven", Matthew 6:20. In addition, in Matthew 19:21, Christ told the rich young ruler to give his possessions to the poor and he would have treasure in heaven. This book and some of my others, is my work that I am laying up in heaven. I am using my talent of writing to share what I have learned from God's word so that it might help others and increase their faith. "Faith comes by hearing, and hearing by the word of God," Romans 10:17. If my writing helps you, then you, too, can use my words to tell and share it with others. This way you can share in the work I do and my work will be part of your works and the Lord will reward you when He returns.

I am also writing this book to give insight into some of the hidden mysteries of the Bible. Many today say they want to know God and have a closer walk with Him; but is this true? I will challenge you to follow God and not man. For Christ Himself said, "If you love father, mother, brother or sister more than me, you are not worthy to follow me", Matthew 10:37.

I am going to try to explain some of the things that I've discovered over the years in studying the Scriptures. I have been seeking for the truth since I was fourteen years old (which was in 1965). Christ says in His word, *"Seek and you shall find; knock and it shall be open unto you."* If you *truly look* for the truth, you can find it. You must listen to what the Word says, however, and not to any man, a church or even a world leader. If you question something that I have written, look for yourselves. Christ is the truth, so you cannot go wrong in following Him.

Most of the quotes I will be using are from the King James Version of the Bible, although I used several translations, along with the Interlinear Bible with Greek/Hebrew/English translations for my research.

Do not read this book unless you have an open heart and really want to know the truth. Even then, you may be upset for a short time. This is because it is difficult to learn that you have been wrong about some things and must make changes if you wish to follow God. I remember, long ago, reading something that was true, but I didn't like it because it showed me that I was wrong in what I had been doing. I actually became angry for a while. Then God convicted my heart. I had asked to know the truth, and then when He began to show me, I didn't like it. Later, as I reflected on these things, I came to realized that I must follow Him and not man or any of man's traditions if I was to please Him. Likewise, if you have the right kind of heart, God will lead you and show you His truth, not necessarily what people have told you.

In this book of sixty-two thousand words, I will discuss topics such as, is the Lord going to physically return to the earth and if so, how and when? What happens when you die? Who are the two witnesses the Bible mentions and where are they today? Who is the Antichrist? Did Jesus mean what He said in the Gospels when said in one Scripture, "If you have the faith as a grain of mustard seed you can say unto this mountain be removed and it will obey you," yet no one has ever even come close to doing this. Did He lie? If not, what did He mean? What is God's name?

When was Christ born? When did Christ die? When was He resurrected, plus several other topics that may surprise you?

As I said, do not read this book unless you truly have an open mind and want to know the truth. The Bible says, "The truth will make you free," John 8:32. Therefore, if you wish to have a deeper understanding of the Scriptures and God, then read on.

There is a lot of misinformation about what Christ said. Over the years, man has changed and instituted his own "traditions" the same as they had done in the Lord's time. He said, ***"In vain do you worship me, teaching as doctrines the traditions of men,"*** Matthew 6:7, Mark 7:7, and 15:9. Therefore, I will not "sugar coat" what I write. Galatians 6:7 says, "Be not deceived, God is not mocked: for whatsoever a man sows that shall he also reap."

In reading this, you will soon see that I have used the name that the Lord was given before His birth by the angel that appeared to Mary. It is also the name He was given when He was eight days old at His circumcision ceremony. The name He was given and used was and is, **Yeshua**. Mel Gibson's movie, *The Passion of the Christ,* also used His Hebrew name. The Hebrew name, Yeshua, means **Salvation**! The letters of the name also mean something. At the end of this book, I have Christ's name spelled out. Each letter in the Hebrew alphabet stands for a word and the letters in His name says it all! Therefore, at the end of this book I have one other mystery. The Bible says in Acts 4:12, "There is no other name given unto men by which they might be saved." Therefore, His name must be important. If you read the first King James Bibles that were translated in 1611, the name Jesus is not in them. It was then spelled Iesus and this was a change from Yeshua. I explain this more a little later.

I have just completed a book called *A Rude Awakening.* It goes into more detail about what most believe will be the "rapture." Most Christians believe that there will a "secret rapture" and they will instantaneously be gone to heaven. When this happens, many of their loved ones and all of the wicked will be left behind on the earth to suffer a "Great Tribulation." There have even been popular movies depicting this. Nonbelievers, of course, do not believe any of this and they often ridicule and make fun of those that do. Both, however, are in for *a rude awakening*, because both are very wrong!

In my book **"Christ: His Words, His Life"** I have much of this at the end in my commentary called "Food for Thought". If you wish to read the four Gospels woven into one, I suggest you read this one. It is written to make it easier to read and understand and is written like any other novel.

Why am I qualified to write this book? I have studied the Holy Bible and what God has said since I was fourteen-years-old. I am now over 64-years of age and I am also a church ordained Messianic Rabi. That means a "teacher" that believes that Christ was and is not only the Savior of Christians but also the Messiah of the Jews and all other humans on earth. I follow God and not what man has said.

I have also recently, 2015, written several new books that give insight of how God views some controversial topics that we are facing today. *Thou Shall Not Kill: What does God think about the killing of animals*, addresses the subject is it wrong to kill certain animals for sport or for food and why. Another of my books is called *ABORTION: Why the Controversy?* What does the Bible say about this? Another is a book I titled *That's Bellabuggery: What in the world does that mean?* This title came from a vision I had where I saw nothing, but heard a voice speak that very odd word. Later, I came to understand that a previous dream, I had two weeks before, was also a vision because they meant the same thing. In the first dream, I was shown something and told what it was. I soon discovered that these two dreams, which both had strange words spoken, was a prophecy that was to come to pass twenty-three years later. The dreams came in 1992 and the visions were concerning homosexual marriage and the state the world would be in at that time.

I have also recently written *Gun Control: What is the answer?* I have been an outdoor writer for many years and I write about hunting, fishing and conservation. I have also studied the Bible for fifty years and this is why I wrote the book.

The last book is, I believe, my greatest work. I named it *Madam President* and the main author is Veronica Fox. When you finish the story, you will understand why she wrote the book and why I am the co-author. It is a 93,000-word novel about the first woman president of the United States. She wins with the new Constitutional Party because the country gets fed up with all the bickering and strife of the two major parties.

Catherine Ann MacIntyre is a down to earth woman that was raised on an Illinois farm. By her wit and charm, she is elected by a landslide. If you think that Donald Trump is outspoken, she makes him look like a little shy boy, although with more wit and charm.

She has bulldog determination and a strong faith in God. She also has three women bodyguards, one of which ends up having a romantic relationship with a man she meets at the President's farm.

This story has drama, humor, romance and heart touching moments. She also becomes friends with a preacher that becomes her spiritual adviser and he is quite a bit like her. He does not care if he is politically correct, for he follows God not man.

I believe this book could change the course this country is on, for if it does not change soon it will be too late, if it is not already too late to turn it around. We all need to pray for our country and do what we can to have God bless it again. Persecution against Christians has already begun in America and it will get worse. We need to pull together if we are to make a change. If this last book were made into a movie, it could change America. Please check it out and tell others. The book you are reading is the most popular I have ever written. *Madam President* is the fifth, but even at that, few are being sold or read.

Chapter 1

The Foundation

Before you build a house, you must have a foundation. The Lord gave a parable of the wise man and a foolish one, Matthew 7:24-27. The first built his house on a rock. The second built his on sand. When the storms and rains came, the man that built his house on sand suffered a great loss. The man, however, that had built his house on a rock suffered no loss. The same goes for building up your knowledge of the Holy Scriptures. If you do not have a solid foundation when tests come, (and they will), everything you have learned may crumble and fall. When this happens, it can leave you disillusioned and confused. It can even make you lose your faith. Matthew 13:20-22 shows this can happen.

First, build your foundation on the Rock, which is Christ. How do you do this? Learn who He was and is. Most do not even know who Christ is.

Let us go back to the beginning to see who He was and is. **"In the beginning was the Word and the Word was with God and the Word was God, and the Word became flesh and dwelt among us,"** John 1:1- and John 1:14.

This is very clear. The Word became Christ. Christ is Greek for "The Anointed One". If you have ever seen a movie or been to a synagogue, you may have seen a Rabbi carrying the Torah scroll (the first five books of the Bible) in his arms. He cradles this "Word" with care and reverence as you would a baby, which is a perfect picture of Christ as an infant.

To understand God's word, you must see things as He sees them, not as man does. God has had a plan since the foundation of the world. He is not confused or in the dark about anything. He knows the end from the beginning, Isaiah 46:10. There is nothing that takes Him by surprise. Everything goes according to His plan. This is not to say that He wishes bad things to happen to good people. On the contrary, he said, "It must needs be, that offenses come, but woe to those that bring the offenses," Matthew 18:7 and Luke 17:1.

To see things as God does, you must understand what His overall plan is. I explain more of this later, but I will give a brief overview now. After the fall of man, God chose certain men to bring about His plan to save human kind from eternal death. Then with Abraham He chose his son Isaac and then Jacob. After this, He chose Jacob's twelve sons who would be the twelve tribes of Israel. Jacob's name was later changed to Israel. Out of the twelve tribes, God chose Juda, which became known as the Jews. With this tribe, Christ was born to bring about His plan of redemption and salvation of the entire world.

Christ said, "No one takes my life. I lay it down of myself. And if I lay it down, I have the power to pick it up again," John 10:17-18.

His purpose for being born was to die for the sins of the world and to reconcile man to God. This, however, is only part of His plan, for there is much more.

To fully understand the Scriptures and how God is working out His plan to bring His Kingdom to earth, you must first understand what He told Israel. He gave a blueprint of His plans to ancient Israel. Most think that the Old Testament does not mean much to a Christian today. Nothing could be farther from the truth. Without the Old Testament, you have no foundation. God shows His entire plan of salvation, redemption, the resurrection and His kingdom being set up on the earth through the Old

Testament. Christ did not have the New Testament and neither did any of the early Christians. All they had was God's word, which was what we now call the Old Testament. Most of the things in the New Testament are quotes from the Old Testament or explanations about what was meant by these Scriptures. Apostle Paul explains many things that shed light on passages from the Old Testament and how they pertain to our lives today and will in the future.

I will explain more in later chapters because there is no way I can say everything in one chapter that needs to be said. It will take the entire book to explain everything so you will understand all that needs to be understood. Even then, you will continue to learn as God opens up more understanding from day to day.

The most important thing is to ask God to open your heart and mind and let Him guide you. If you are Jew or gentile, God will open your eyes if you want Him to. He said no one can come to me (Christ) unless the Father draws them, John 6:44 and John 6:65. Apostle Paul said in Romans 3:1-2, "What advantage has a Jew? Much in every way: chiefly because unto them were committed the oracles of God."

After the Lord returns and sets up His Kingdom on earth, the Bible tells us in Zechariah 8:23, "In those days it shall come to pass, that ten men from different languages of the nations, shall take hold of the skirt of a Jew saying, "We will go with you, for we have heard that God is with you."

Therefore, if we look at what God has told the Jews and all of Israel, then we can understand what He has also told the Christians. Many of the parables that Christ told do not make much sense unless you understand them from a Jewish perspective. Other Scriptures do not make much sense unless you understand what God is trying to do. Today, God is beginning to open up the Scriptures in a way He never has before. As He said in Daniel 12, knowledge shall be increased in the latter days. As time ticks down, more and more will be revealed, but at the same time, more and more people will not care to understand. If you read the book of Revelation you will see that the hearts of most will be very hard when God finally intervenes in human affairs. People will not want God in their lives and they will become very angry at Him, even when He tries to save them from their own self-destruction.

Chapter 2

What was the Name Given to Christ?

As I said earlier, the Bible says the Word became flesh and dwelt among us. In Genesis 1:26, God said, "Let **US** make man in **Our** likeness and in Our image." In this, you can see that the Word was with God and was God.

Later, when Abraham went to Salem, which would later be known as Jerusalem, he met with Melchizedek. Melchizedek was "the high priest of the Most High God." This account is in Genesis 14:18. This is Christ before He was in the flesh. Apostle Paul tells us this in Hebrews 5:10, (Christ was) "Called of God a high priest after the order of Melchizedek."

Christ was also in the fiery furnace in Daniel 3:25, "…and the form of the fourth (man) is like the Son of God."

The Lord Himself said when speaking of His Father in John 5:37, "You have neither heard His voice at any time, nor seen His shape."

This makes it perfectly clear that anytime God spoke in the Old Testament it was the Word speaking, which later became Christ. Christ was with the Israelites in the desert for the forty years they were there, and it was He that spoke to Moses. 1 Corinthians 10:4, "…the spiritual Rock that followed them, and that Rock was Christ."

Now that we know the Word was and is God, was with God from the beginning and later became Christ in the flesh, we can begin to understand the Scriptures better.

One of most surprising revelations is that the name given to the baby Christ was not Jesus.

First, let me say that I was saved when I believed His name was Jesus. I prayed to Him believing that this was His name and I'm sure He heard me. A child cannot say their father's name correctly at first, but the father knows that the child is talking to him. My first words where Da-Da, but my father knew I was trying to say Daddy. The Bible says, "We cry Abba, Father," Mark 14:36, Romans 8:15 and Galatians 4:6. Abba means a more intimate name we would call our father, such as Daddy.

As I said earlier, the first King James Bibles were printed in 1611 and the word Jesus is not in it. Even James did not have a J yet. The J was added later. His name in the first King James Bible began with an I. It was Iesus. The name Christ was given at birth was Yeshua. What's in a name you might ask? The children of the Bible were named for something they were to do, become or the parent wanted them to be. The first translators changed the Y of Yeshua's name into the letter I, but it still had the Y sound. Then they added an S on the end to give it a more masculine sound. They did this on many biblical names. Juda was often translated Judas. The original name, however, was Yehuda. Jerusalem was Yerushalayim.

The Lord's earthly name that He was given during the circumcision ceremony on His eighth day of life was Yeshua. It means **salvation** and anytime you read the word *salvation* in the Bible, you can put His name in that sentence and the Bible shows you even more how He saves us. When you get to the end of this book and read, *"What's in a Name?"* you will be awestruck. I know I was the first time I saw it. The reason is that the letters of His name spell out what He was going to do and has done!

Chapter 3

Who was Christ and why was He Born?

I will repeat once again who Christ was. **"In the beginning was the Word and the Word was with God and the Word was God and the Word became flesh and dwelt among us."**

In Genesis, God said, "Let **Us** make man in **Our** image after **Our** likeness." God is a Spirit and His Word is a part of Him. It is difficult for us to understand exactly what a spirit is. The Lord explained to Nicodemus, that night when he spoke with Him, that a spirit is invisible, at least it is to us. We have mortal eyes, but spirits could be seen, if we were in the realm they are.

Man was given a test in the Garden of Eden and from the moment that Adam and Eve failed that test, God already had a plan to rescue them and their descendants. If you remember, there was a prophesy that the Lord made in the garden, when He said, "The woman's seed (descendant/ Christ) would crush the head of Satan and Satan's seed would bruise His (Christ's) heal," Genesis 3:15. In the Gospels, the Lord often calls Himself the Son of man. He does this to show that He is not only the Son of God but also the Son of Adam. Adam means "from the earth."

Many do not realize that Christ was here long before He was born as a baby in a manger. He first appeared in human form as Melchizedek when He spoke with Abraham, Genesis 14:18. That is the reason Christ said what He did to the Pharisees, that "Abraham was glad to see Him," and that, "Before Abraham was, I AM," John 8:58. He was also the "Tree of Life" in the Garden of Eden and He was the one that spoke with Adam and Eve.

He was the Rock that followed the children of Israel in the wilderness for forty years, 1 Corinthians 10:4. He was also the "fourth man" in the fiery furnace. He also was the one that spoke to Moses. In fact, any time God has spoken, it was the Word, which was Christ. Sometimes in the Bible, angels spoke God's Words in a vision or in person, but when God spoke, it was His Word (Christ) doing the speaking. Christ Himself said no man has seen the Father at any time, John 6:46.

In my book, *Christ: His Words, His Life*, I wrote that when the Lord was speaking to Peter and said, ***"You are Peter* (the Stone) *and upon this Rock* (Christ) *I will build My church."*** I did this because He was "the Corner Stone that was rejected". He is often referred to as the Rock. He spoke this same way when He said, ***"Destroy 'this Temple' and in three days I will raise it again."*** In addition, the passage that says, **"What you bind on earth has already been bound in heaven"** is the correct translation in Hebrew/Greek. This also makes sense, for even Christ Himself could not change anything that the Father told Him to say or do.

I wrote this passage this way because some today think that Peter had the power to change God's laws and if Peter could change it, then so can the leaders of some churches today. Christ said that "not one jot or tittle of the law shall pass away until all be fulfilled, Matthew 5:18.

Back in the beginning, when man first sinned, God killed an animal and clothed Adam and Eve to "cover" their sin. Later, the "Lamb of God" would be killed to take that sin away. Did you notice what happened in the "Garden of Gethsemane" (Mark 14:51-52), when the young man ran up to the Lord, gave Him a white linen cloth and ran away naked?

Why was this recorded in the Gospels? It is a picture of what happened in the "Garden of Eden," only reversed. Man had lost his eternal life by committing the first sin. Then God killed an animal (probably a lamb) to clothe the first Adam to "cover" his sin, and his nakedness. The young man who was representing an earthly "Adam" handed the Lord, who was representing a spiritual Adam, a pure, white linen *covering,* and left naked. The white linen represents purity and Christ (the Lamb of God) was getting ready to die and take away all of man's sins, including this young man's. This was done to give man back eternal life; which Adam had lost.

Who was this young man? Do you remember the rich young ruler that came and fell down before the Lord and worshiped Him and said, "Good Master, what must I do to inherent eternal life?" The Lord told him to keep the commandments, and the young man said that he had kept them since he was a child. The scripture also says, "Yeshua looked at him and loved him." Then the Lord told him to go and sell everything he had and give the money to the poor, Matthew 19:21 and Luke 18:22.

I believe this young man did exactly that. He would not have kept the commandments if he did not love God. I also believe that since he loved God, he thought about what the Lord had told him, and then went and sold everything he had, except for that piece of linen cloth. Then he even gave that away, (to the Lord) and had "nothing" on this earth; although he had treasure in heaven, as the Lord told him he would. By the young man doing this, it is a picture of what had happened in the Garden of Eden, only in reverse. The curse that man had been under for centuries was being undone! God had clothed the "first Adam" with a bloody skin after he had sinned. Now a descendant of the first Adam was giving God back a "covering" that was pure and white. The "Last Adam" (Christ) who would soon be "made a quickening spirit," 1 Corinthians 15:45, was becoming the "lamb" that had been skinned to cover Adam and Eve. Christ's body would be like the bloody skin that would not only be covering their sin, but would also be taking it away forever. Fine "linen, white and clean," Revelation 3:5 -6, Revelation 6:11, 19:8 and 19:14, would now replace the skin given by God in the Garden of Eden. This white linen clothing represents righteousness. We are not righteous, but Christ was "without sin" and was the "perfect sacrifice" so that He could pay the price to redeem us. "We have been bought with a price," 1 Corinthians 6:20 and 7:23.

Chapter 4

Did God do away with The Ten Commandments?

What did the Lord say when the rich young ruler came and asked, "Good Master, what must I do to inherent eternal life?" Christ said, ***"Keep the Commandments!"*** This is in Matthew 19:17 and Luke 18:21. He also said, ***"I have not come to change the law but fulfill it."*** Again, He said, ***"Not one jot or tittle of the law will be done away with until all are fulfilled,"*** Matthew 5:17-18. Many will say, "God 'nailed the law' to the cross!" No, He didn't, He "nailed" *the penalty of the law*, which was against us, Colossians 2:14. Just as the woman that was caught in the act of adultery was worthy of the penalty of death, He came to bring forgiveness and a time of "Grace" until He returns. She was worthy to die as many or most are today. We do not have to sacrifice animals any longer to cover our sins, because He was "the perfect sacrifice," and His sacrifice does not cover sins but takes them away, if we are sincere and ask Him to forgive us. What did He say about forgiveness? We must forgive those that ask us to forgive them. In addition, if we have done someone wrong, we must go to him or her and ask them for forgiveness. God will forgive you but first you must ask Him, otherwise your sin remains. If you have harmed someone else, you must ask their forgiveness first, before you go to God to ask His forgiveness, or how else will the people you have wronged know that you are sorry.

God gave His Commandments not to be a burden on us, but to give us a happier, healthier life. Just think how great our lives would be, if everyone on earth followed God's "rules."

It is much easier to understand if I explain it in terms of today. Think of God's laws as traffic laws. Traffic laws are there to keep us safe. It is unlawful to not stop at a stop sign or run a red light. It is unlawful to pass on a sharp curve or going over a hill where you cannot see oncoming traffic. There are yellow lines on the road or signs that say, "Do Not Pass." There are many traffic laws and "they were written" for our good and welfare. This was the same purpose that God had His laws "written". Since Christ died as the "final sacrifice", there is no longer a "penalty of the law". It would be like if suddenly all the traffic laws would not be enforced and you would not be fined or put in jail for any violation. You could run stop signs, red lights, speed, hit and kill pedestrians and never face any charges. Can you imagine the chaos? There would be death and destruction everywhere if no one followed the laws that were once in place. If, however, people obeyed the traffic laws, even if there were no penalties, everything would be fine.

If the "traffic laws" were never written, how would we know how to follow the "rules of the road"? This was why God wrote His laws. Without them, we would not know how to do what He wishes us to do, or what is best for us. Therefore, if you do not obey God's laws, there may not be a penalty during this life, but He will hold you accountable later.

In Old Testament times, most people obeyed God's laws out of fear of the penalties. Today God wants us to obey His laws because we know they are the right thing to do. He also wants us to do them because we love Him. His laws are to be written on our hearts and God judges the heart.

If you read in the last book of the Bible, you will find that God expects us to keep His Commandments. Revelation 12:17 says, "And the dragon (Satan) was angry with the woman and went to make war with the rest of her seed, which **keep the Commandments of God** and have the testimony of Christ."

In addition, in the last chapter, of the last book of the Bible, it says the same thing. Revelation 22:14 says, "Blessed are they that **do His Commandments**!"

This shows beyond a doubt, that the Lord expects us, His followers, to keep His Commandments and love one another. So, the answer to the question, did God do away with the Ten Commandments is, **NO!**

Chapter 5

What did Christ Preach?

What did Christ preach when He began His ministry? He preached the Gospel. What is the Gospel? The Gospel means Good News. What was the Good News? The Good News was and is that God was sending His Son to take away our sins and to give us eternal life. It was also to give us hope that when we die, we would live again and forever in His Kingdom. What is His Kingdom that He spoke of so much? Remember the Lord's Prayer, *"Thy Kingdom come, thy will be done, on earth as it is in heaven."*

Christ told many parables about the Kingdom, often comparing it to a field of planted seed and a harvest. This is a very good analogy. The Apostle Paul said in 2 Corinthians 15:35-54, that when we die, we are like a seed that is put in the ground, and when we come up, we look totally different than we did before we went in. We will be raised with a spiritual body that cannot die. The Lord, in the book of Revelation talks about reaping the harvest. The Lord came and planted the first seed of the Gospel and it has grown since that time, just like the parable of the mustard seed.

Remember He said the Kingdom does not "come" with observation, Luke 17:20. However, a few lines down, He said He would return to this earth to set up His Kingdom. When He first came, the Kingdom was invisible to man, for the kingdom was Christ Himself and the Spirit that was inside of Him. That's why in my book *CHRIST: His Words, His Life,* when I came to the verse His "Kingdom comes without observation" I put "begins" instead of comes; it is understandable then. When something first appears, it often is invisible to the human eye. Therefore, when something "first comes," it also begins.

Why were you born? What is the purpose of man? If you listen to His words, it becomes clear. We were made in the image of God. God is an invisible spirit, yet we have God-like qualities. We can love and that is the greatest gift of God, for He is love. We not only can love one another, we can love God and we can know and feel God's love. When you look into another person's eyes, you are looking into the face of God because we were made in His image. The eyes are the window to the soul, or the innermost being. Most do not understand that we are also "joint heirs" with Christ! Everything in the universe belongs to Christ because He said He created everything. Think about it. If God, at one time, gave the earth to Lucifer (Satan), why wouldn't He give us as much or more? Remember when Christ was tempted by Satan and Satan told him, "All the kingdoms of the earth are mine. They were given to me and I have the right to give them to you and I will, if you bow down and worship me," Matthew 4:8 and Luke 4:5.

God has billions of galaxies, in each galaxy are billions of stars, and around many of those stars are planets. In 1 Corinthians 2:9 it says, "Eye has not seen nor ear heard, neither has entered into the heart of man, the things which God has prepared for them that love Him." He even says in His word, that we will "judge angels", 1 Corinthians 6:3, and we will rule the earth with Him when He returns. After this thousand-year rule of the earth, He will create a new heaven and a new earth and He will live with us forever. I will explain more on this later because many do not understand what this really is.

So, what is the purpose of man? God is creating children for Himself. God is an Echad, which is Hebrew for several that are one. The Bible speaks of this a lot. In Genesis it says, **"Let Us make man."** Yet the Bible says,

"Hear O Israel, the Lord our God is one Lord!" This is why many of the Jews, in the time of Christ, could not understand how He could be the Son of God. They could not see that He had come before, but in a different form. There are many members of a church, yet one body. Our bodies have many members: hands, feet, eyes, ears, mouth and so forth, yet it is one body. Most know about the God Head. It is difficult for us to understand spiritual things; it is hard enough to understand earthly things. I try to see God as an analogy of water. Water can be in three forms; ice as a solid form; water as a liquid form and vapor as a gaseous form. It is still the same water, but in different forms and in different places.

Chapter 6

What Happens when you Die?

Most do not know or understand what happens when you die, but the Word of God is very clear on this subject if you take the time to read it. Many take a couple of passages that can be read contrary to all the others and base their belief on them. However, you must take the Scriptures that are very clear and see if the few that are not so clear line up with them and they do. The way we see things and the way God sees things are very different. He said, in Isaiah 55:8-9, "For my thoughts are not your thoughts, neither are your ways my ways, says the LORD. For as the heavens are higher than the earth, so are my ways higher than your ways and my thoughts than your thoughts."

God made life and He knows all things concerning life and Death. When Christ died on the cross He said, ***"Father, into your hands I commend my spirit."*** Christ did not go to heaven at that time because He was in the tomb for three days and three nights, Matthew 12:40. Christ was also different from anyone else because He had the power to raise Himself. He said in John 10:18, "No one takes my life from me. I have the power to lay it down and I have the power to pick it up again." We, however, will have to wait until He raises us at the resurrection. How do we know this? He tells us plainly and I will quote Him and the Apostles to show you.

When God made man, He "breathed the breath of life" into him and when you die, that "breath of life" goes back to God. Adam was complete, but he was not conscious before

God put that "breath" into him. Some think this is just air but I believe it is more; it is an energy, a life force. No one can completely understand how God will join our new spiritual resurrected body with our personality; the things that makes us who we are. Every cell in our body has a complete blueprint of us. I am sure there is also a blueprint that is stamped on a spiritual "cell" somewhere that is in God's control. It may be something like a DVD disk that has everything about us down to our thoughts, memories and feelings. Then when it is put into our new body, we are complete. A computer disk or other disk can be put into any player and we can have all the information transferred to the other player. Without a devise (a body), it is just information stored on a disk.

Everything in the universe is made up of atoms and these are held together with energy. It is not difficult to believe that there is an energy somewhere, which has all the information about us stored on it. The Lord Himself said that He was "going away to prepare a place for us." Most think this is a "mansion in heaven", but besides creating a new heaven and new earth that we will have someday, He was talking about our new body, our "temple." Remember He said in John 2:19, "Destroy this temple and in three days I will raise it up." He had a *new temple*, a new *body* after He was resurrected. When He returns, we will live with Him for a thousand years on earth. It seems to me that He will bring our new spiritual bodies with Him and the blueprint stored here on earth will be joined to make us complete. In 1 Corinthians 3:16, he says our body is the temple for the Holy Spirit. When He returns, He will be sending out His angels to gather His elect, so I believe the angels will "clothe" us with our new temple (or body). The wicked will be raised at the end of the thousand years, but they will not have a spiritual body, they will be in a mortal body because they will die the "second death". We that have a spiritual body cannot die again, Revelation 20:6, "on such, the second death has no power."

The book of Isaiah made it clear that there is to be a resurrection. Isa 26:19, "But **your dead will live**; their bodies will rise. You, who dwell in the dust, wake up and shout for joy. Your dew is like the dew of the morning; **the earth will give birth to her dead**."

Here are some passages in the Bible about death and they speak for themselves. After these, I will talk about the few that some people take and "twist around" so that they contradict all the others. Therefore, read for yourself what God says in His Word about death:

Genesis 3:19, "Dust you are and **dust you shall return**."

Psalm 13:3, "Lest I sleep the **sleep of death**."

Psalm 16:9-10, "Therefore, my heart is glad; **my flesh** also **shall rest in hope**. "For you will not leave my soul in hell (the grave), neither will you suffer your Holy One to see corruption." (Speaking of Christ)

Psalm 17:15, "I shall be satisfied, **when I awake with your likeness!"**

Psalm 30: 9, "What profit is there in my blood (death) when I go down to the pit. Shall the dust praise you?"

Psalm 48:14-15, "Like sheep that are laid in the grave, their beauty shall consume in the grave. But **God will redeem my soul from the power of the grave**, for He shall receive me."

Psalm 50:5, "**Gather My saints together unto Me**, those that have made a covenant with me by sacrifice."

Psalm 68:22, "**I will bring again my people from the depths of the sea**."

Psalm 71:20, "You shall **quicken me again** and shall bring me up again **from the depths of the earth!"**

Psalm 88:10-11, "Will you show wonders to the dead? Shall your loving kindness be declared in the grave?"

Psalm 94:17, "Unless the Lord had been my help, my soul had almost dwelt in silence."

Psalm 116:15, "Precious in the sight of the Lord is the death of His saints."

Psalm 114:17, "**The dead praise not the Lord**, neither any that go down in silence."

Psalm 139:8, "If I make my bed in hell (the grave), behold you are there."

Psalm 143:3, "He has made me to dwell in darkness, as those that have been long dead."

Psalm 146:4, "His breath goes forth, **he returns to his earth**; in that very day, **his thoughts perish.**"

Daniel 12:2, "Many of them that **sleep in the dust** of the earth **shall awake.**"

Daniel 12:13, "For you shall rest and stand in your lot at the end of the days."

John 11:11, "Our friend Lazarus is *sleeping,* but I go that I may *awake him* out of his sleep."

John 11:23-24, "Thy brother shall arise again. . .. **He shall arise in the resurrection at the last day.**"

1 Corinthians 15:6, "But some are fallen **asleep.**"

1 Corinthians 15:20, "Christ is risen from the dead and become the **"first fruits"** of them that **sleep.**"

1 Corinthians 15:22-23, "For **in Adam all die**, even so **in Christ shall all be made alive.**" "But **every man in his order**; Christ the first fruits; and afterward **they** that are Christ's *at His coming."*

1 Corinthians 15:42, "So also the resurrection of the dead. It is **sown in corruption**; it is **raised** in **incorruption.**"

1 Corinthians 15:51-52, "We shall not all sleep (die), but we shall all be changed; in a moment, in the twinkling of an eye." . . . "Dead shall be raised."

John 3:13, "**No man has ascended up to heaven**, but He that came down from heaven, even the Son of Man."

John 3:15, "That whosoever believes in Him should not perish but have eternal life."

Acts 2:29, "David that he is both dead and buried.

Acts 2:34, "For **David has not ascended into the heavens**."

These seem very clear that when you die you go to sleep and stay asleep in death until Christ returns. He then sends His angels with a great sound of a trumpet (the last or seventh) and wakes the dead and they are gathered unto Him. We have a spiritual body at that time, "for flesh and blood cannot inherit the Kingdom of God," 1 Corinthians 15:50.

In Matthew 24: 31 and Mark 13:41, it says that He will send out His angels and they will gather His elect. In 2 Thessalonians, it says, "The dead in Christ shall rise first and then we which are alive and remain shall be changed and *caught up* to meet the Lord in the air." Who catches you? The angels, as He said in Matthew.

What does it mean in the Bible when it says, "Death delivered up the dead who was in it," Revelation 20:13. This simply means that those which have died by being totally destroyed, as in fire or eaten by an animal or completely turned to ashes or dust, so as there are no more mortal remains.

Some people think that if you have 'treasure in heaven' it means you go there when you die, or how else will you receive your reward. Revelation 22:12 states, "My reward is with me, to give to every man according to his work shall be."

Are there any Scriptures that say, "When you die you go straight to heaven?" No, there is no such Scripture anywhere in the Bible. What we have read so far says that when you die, your body turns back to dust; and when the Lord returns on "the last day," you will be resurrected, just as He was resurrected.

What about the Scripture in Revelation 6:9-11? It says, "I saw the souls of them that were killed for the Word of God under the altar." This was a vision the Apostle John was given. He was seeing a symbolic event. The ones crying out were asking the Lord how long it would be before He punished those living on earth, for they were killed by the wicked for their faith. God said in Genesis 4:10, that Abel's blood also "cried out." These people in Revelation (and Abel was among them) were told to "rest a little season" until their brothers were also killed. This "little season" is the time the Great Tribulation takes millions of Christian lives, the last 42 months before Christ returns.

One other Scripture people use to "prove" that a person goes to heaven as soon as they die is the "parable" of Lazarus and the rich man, Luke 16:20-31. Listen carefully at what it says, "Lazarus died and was "carried by angels" to Abraham. Now where have we heard that before? When Christ returns, He will send out His angels and they will "gather" His saints just as the Bible says in Matthew 24 and Mark 13.

Where will they be taken? They will be gathered to the Lord with all the other saints. Now Father Abraham is the father of all that is of the promise. God had promised him that his descendants would be as numerous as the stars in heaven. He was the father of the nation of Israel and of Ishmael, who became the father of many Arab nations and people. The greatest number of people, however, was to be the *children of promise*, because when Christ came and died, all nations could come and be part of His Kingdom.

Now the other part of the parable was that later, the rich man died and in "hell" (verse 23) lifted up his eyes. What does this mean? Hell was the grave. We all go to the grave and later everyone that has ever lived will be raised. ***It is appointed unto men once to die and after this the judgment,*** Hebrews 9:27. 'Lifted up his eyes' means when he awoke from death; he was not carried by angels as was

Lazarus. There are **two resurrections** as told in Revelation 20:5-6. The first is for the righteous at the Lord's return, and the second is for the wicked or those that die during the millennium. The rich man had no consciousness in the grave and he was unaware that centuries had passed. In fact, the first resurrection happens a thousand years before the second; this span of one-thousand years is the "gulf" that is fixed between them.

Another Scripture people use to "prove" a person goes directly to heaven is the incident of the thief on the cross. The thief asked the Lord, "Remember me when you come into your Kingdom," Luke 23:42. When was Christ "coming" into His Kingdom? When He returns to earth, He resurrects His saints and then sets up His Kingdom, Revelation 20:6. The Lord replied to him and said, "I tell you this day (right now), you shall be with me in Paradise." When this was written, there were no punctuation marks, so there was no comma in the sentence. The thief could not have gone to heaven that day, because Christ did not go to heaven at that time. He said He would be in the grave for "three days and three nights," Matthew 12:40. What is Paradise? It means a beautiful garden, like Eden, a place of pleasure and comfort, as when He sets up His Kingdom on earth. That is what Christ promised him.

We did not get tired of waiting to be born the first time, and we will have no idea how much time has passed after we die, until we are resurrected. Job said in Job 14:13-14, "O if you would hide me in the grave, if you would keep me secret until Your wrath be past, if You would appoint me a *set time*, and remember me. If a man dies, shall he live again? All the days of my *appointed time* will I wait, until my *change* come." This "change" happens at the resurrection, 1 Corinthians 15:51-52, "We shall all be changed." The word change also means a metamorphosis, or a transformation into something else such as a caterpillar into a butterfly. This "change" that Job spoke of was the same one that every child of God will go through in the resurrection on the "last day" and this day will be on a "set time' that only God knows, Matthew 24:36. Therefore, it will seem like it is but a few seconds from the time we die, until we awake. When you are put to sleep when you have surgery, you cannot tell if you have been asleep for ten minutes or ten hours. It will be the same when you die. This way, the ones that have died centuries ago will awaken at the same time as the ones that have just recently passed away. How marvelous are God's ways!

What did Christ mean when He said in Matthew 22:32 and Luke 20:38, "God is not God of the dead, but of the living?"

To God, we do not die, we "fall asleep", for He has the power to wake us. That is why He said what He did about His friend Lazarus when he died, John 11:11. Christ said Lazarus was *asleep* and that He was going to go and wake him. The disciples thought by this statement that Lazarus was sleeping and getting needed rest. The Lord then told them plainly, "he is dead." Also, when He came to Martha, He asked her, "Will he live again?" and Martha said, "Yes, Lord, in the resurrection at the *last day,*" John 11:24.

In Acts 7:55-56, when Stephen is about to be stoned to death, he is given a vision of heaven and Christ is seen on the right hand of God. It is not out of the question that as soon as you die and before you go to sleep in death that you could have a vision. God could also speak to you and prepare you for the resurrection. He is not a God of confusion but of peace and order, 1 Corinthians 14:33. There have been many that have died in terrible accidents, wars or been martyred, where the person may wake up in the resurrection and be confused or frightened. God has the power to speak even to the dead (as He did Lazarus when He raised him) and to comfort those that are His. This may be why people that have died for a few minutes have had out of body experiences, have seen things and then been revived to live to tell about it.

It is clear that Christ had to be the *first* to be resurrected, because He was the "first fruits." The rest of His brothers that sleep, as He did, will be resurrected when He returns, 1 Corinthians 15:20. All of His followers will be raised on that last day, John 6:39, 40, 44 and 54.

If you lose a spouse to death, as I did, and they are still alive in heaven, how can you remarry? Can you imagine how awful it would be if you died and went to heaven and could see what was happening on earth and another man married your wife? You would have to know he was making love to her and that is if he was a good man. Some could mistreat her or your children. It would not be heaven if you saw some of the terrible things going on to your loved ones. That is why God said, "The dead know nothing."

In addition, on that "last day," many people that we think of as being great saints, may not be to God and may not be raised in the first resurrection. Do you remember when Christ's brothers, sisters and mother were outside wanting to see Him, Matthew 12:48 and Mark 3:33? He said, *"Who is my mother, my brother, my sister?"* He made this clear that we are just as important as His earthly mother, His earthly brothers and sisters or His friends. He also said, "Many that are first shall be last and the last first," Matthew 19:30 and Mark 10:31. He was the one that died for us and no one else can give you eternal life; He is the "Way; the Truth; and the Life," John 14:16. In Revelation 5:2-5, it says there was no one on earth, under the earth, or in heaven that was worthy to open the seals, except Christ. He is our mediator between the Father and us. There is no one else that can fill that position.

What was the Mount of Transfiguration? Read carefully in Matthew 17:9 it says, "Tell the *vision* to no man." This was a "vision," it was not real. Moses had already died; Christ had not yet been resurrected and glorified. This was

only a vision. Moses was not there alive speaking with Him. I did not mention Elijah here, but I will talk about him later.

Here are Christ's own words in John 5:25 and 28 *"Do not marvel at this; for the hour is coming, in which ALL that are in the graves will hear His voice, and shall come out; they that have done good unto the resurrection of life; and they that have done evil, unto the resurrection of damnation."* This makes it very clear where the dead are. The dead are not in heaven or Christ would bring them with him, He would not have to call them forth from the grave. In addition, if they were in heaven, He would have told you; He would not have said the opposite.

No, we will not go directly to heaven when we die. When the "rapture" takes place those that are dead will rise first and we that are alive and remain will be changed and "caught up" by angels to Christ. Christ will be in the air. I explain more on this later.

Note: I have written a new book, which goes into more detail about what happens when you die. It was published in May 2017 and it is tilted, "What Happens When You Die? Is there Life after Death?"

Chapter 7

God's Holy Days

You do not get a clear picture of why the Lord returns and what happens when He does without understanding what God's Holy Days are. By understand these, you will then understand God's timetable.

I also need to mention that 'holiday' is derived from 'holy day'. Most holidays that Christians celebrate are in no way connected to God's Holy Days. You will see what I mean as I now explain.

What are God's Holy Days and what do they mean? God, in His wisdom, gave us a blueprint for His entire plan of redemption, His Kingdom to be set up on earth and His people to be given eternal life. Most think that these days were "given to the Jews" and do not have any bearing on Christians today. Nothing could be farther from the truth.

Let us look at how God "chose" His people. Immediately after Adam and Eve sinned, He promised a Redeemer through their descendants, Genesis 3:15. Then He chose Noah, and sometime later, He chose Abraham to bring about His plan of redemption.

Abraham was the first to be the "father" of many nations, Genesis 17:4 and 5. Out of him came Isaac and, since he was willing to "sacrifice his son" to God (Genesis 22:2-18), God later sacrificed His Son for Abraham's physical and spiritual descendants.

Isaac became the father of Jacob. Later, God changed Jacob's name to **Israel.** This was because he had twelve sons, which became the **twelve tribes** of the nation of Israel.

These twelve sons went to Egypt where Joseph, the youngest, had saved them from the famine along with all of Egypt. Joseph had two sons and these two took over as the tribes in his place, so there were really thirteen. The Levites were the priests, however, and when they came out of Egypt and became part of the nation of Israel, they had cities throughout the nation. The other twelve tribes had land given to them inside the nation. Later, the northern part of Israel rebelled and broke away from the tribes of Judah and Benjamin and even had war with one another, 1 Kings 15:7. In 2 Kings 17:6, the northern "ten tribes" of Israel were taken soon afterwards into captivity by Assyria and were "lost" from view. The tribes of Judah and Benjamin would later be called the land of Judah, and the people that lived there were called Jews. All Jews are Israelites, but not all Israelites are Jews. Just as all Hoosiers are Americans, but not all Americans are Hoosiers.

After the northern tribes were taken out of the picture and "lost," the promise of the Messiah would come from the land of Judah and the Jews. This was already planned centuries in advance. This is why Herod had the children killed when Christ was born. The prophets had said that out of Bethlehem, a King was to come, Micah 5:2. Matthew 2:6 is a quote from Micah 5:2. Bethlehem means (house of bread) for He was the Bread that came down from heaven, John 6:33. He also said, "I am the Bread of Life," John 6:48 and John 6:35. Even in the blessing over food (which has been said since the days of Moses), there is a prophecy of Christ's resurrection, which says, "Blessed are you, O Lord our God, who brings forth 'Bread' from the earth."

Now these Holy Days were first given to all of Israel at the time of Moses. Besides the weekly Sabbath, which was given to all mankind at the creation, there are seven yearly **Holy Days,** and each one is a "rehearsal" of things that **will happen** and/or has happened. They are a **blueprint** of God's plan for all humanity.

These days were first given to all of Israel, or strangers that lived among them, Leviticus 23. Later, after the northern ten tribes of Israel were taken away by Assyria, these Holy Days were only for the Jews. Now they are for the Christians and all of God's people. We Christians have been "grafted" in, Romans 11:24. In addition, when the Lord returns, people from many nations (Zechariah 8:23), will come to the Jews to learn God's ways; for these Holy Days are a picture of God's plan for everyone!

The first Holy day is **PASSOVER (Pesach** in Hebrew). Remember in Egypt that at midnight they had to put the "blood of a lamb" on their doorpost so the "Death Angel" would "pass over" that house and the first-born would not die, Exodus 12:27. They also had to hurry and make bread for their journey from Egypt. Since they did not have time to put leaven in the bread and let it rise, they baked their bread without leaven. This was to become the Feast of Unleavened Bread, Exodus 34:18.

When they were in the wilderness, they were told by Moses, who got his instructions directly from God, to do this every year for all generations. During this time in the wilderness, God added the other Holy Days that they were to keep. They understood the Passover and the Feast of Unleavened Bread in part, because they were delivered from the bondage of slavery, but they could not see the entire picture. The other Holy Days they did not understand at all. They only knew that God had said to keep them.

On the first Passover in Egypt and after they came out of Egypt, Moses was instructed to tell the people how to do the Passover, Exodus 12:3-5. They were to bring a *lamb*, "without blemish," into their homes *four days* ahead of time, Exodus 12:2-6. This was done and was to be continued to be done, on the tenth day of the first month. The first month being Abib or Aviv, which means, "green ear" because this was the month the barley was in the green ear stage. After the Babylonian captivity, the first month was often called

Nisan. This corresponds to around Mid-March to early April of the months we go by today. God had the people to "bring the lamb into their homes". This way, the lamb would become something like a pet, so that when they killed it for the feast, they would feel sad about its death. They were also told to roast it over a fire on a stick (a picture of Christ on a cross or tree). The reason they brought the lamb in four days before Passover was a future picture of Christ coming to His own people four days ahead of time when He rode into Jerusalem on a donkey. Then on Passover, the 14th of the first month, He was killed as the Passover Lamb. This was all planned, for He said, ***"No one takes My life. I have the power to lay it down and I have the power to pick it up again,"*** John 10:18. The "lamb's blood" over the doorpost shows that if you have "His blood" over the doorpost of your heart, it will keep you from dying the "second death," and death will pass over you.

I also want to mention that in Acts 12:4, the King James Bible has the word "Easter." This is a mistranslation and it should be "Passover". The word Passover is translated correctly everywhere else in the Bible except for this one passage. If you look in a Webster's dictionary, it tells you that the name Easter comes from the "dawn goddess" and she was worshipped in spring around the same time. The Roman Church combined the two over three centuries later. This was a pagan holiday and had nothing to do with the Lord's death and resurrection.

Exodus 23:15, "You shall keep the feast of ***unleavened bread***: (you shall eat unleavened bread seven days, as I commanded you, in the time appointed of the month Abib; for in it you came out from Egypt: and none shall appear before me empty:)"

The **FEAST** of **UNLEAVENED BREAD (Hag haMatzot** in Hebrew) begins the day following Passover; it is a *High Sabbath*, Exodus 12:15-20. This is why Christ had to be taken down from the cross before sunset. It was the High Sabbath of the Feast of Unleavened Bread that was about to begin, *not the weekly Sabbath* as most people think. God's days begin at sunset and end the next day at sunset.

This Feast of Unleavened Bread was a picture of Christ, being without sin, as leaven represents sin. That is why the custom was, that a few days before this feast, the "Father" of the house had to take a candle or "light" and search the house, even the dark corners, for leaven, (which represented sin) and take it away. Exodus 12:15 says that the "leaven" must be removed from the house before the first day of the Feast of Unleavened Bread. This was why the Lord drove out the moneychangers from "His House", the temple, just before Passover. He was "the Light," Matthew 5:14 and He was taking the leaven out of his Father's house. This was to show us that we need to take the leaven or sin out of our "house" (our temple or body). This is also to show us that we need to search ourselves (our hearts) and get the sin out of our lives.

The Israelites and later just the Jews did this, but they thought it was because of being freed from "bondage" in Egypt. They could not see that it was a picture of Christ coming as "the Lamb of God" to "take away the *sin* of the world," and to free us from the" bondage" of sin.

The unleavened bread is a picture of His body. At the last Passover, which He ate with His disciples, He broke the bread and gave it to them and told them that this was His body, Matthew 26:26, Mark 14:22 and Luke 22:19. If you have seen a piece of this unleavened bread, it is a picture of Him. The bread has tiny holes like piercings; it has dark stripes like whip marks and dark areas that resemble bruising.

There is also a custom that the Jews did and still do at a Passover Saddar, which is a picture of Christ's death, burial and resurrection. They take a piece of the "bread", wrap it in linen cloth and "hide" it. Then the "children" search for it, and when they find it, they "bring it forth" and get a reward. If we search for Christ and find him, we will also get a reward. A reward of eternal life!

The Lord also took the wine that night at the Passover meal and said that it was His blood. In John 6:55-56, He says, "He who eats my flesh and drinks my blood, I dwell in him and he in Me."

At the *Feast of Tabernacles*, which I will talk about later, there is a wine and water pouring ceremony that takes place. In this ceremony, water and wine are poured together onto the ground. This is a perfect picture of the Lord's side being pierced by the spear, with the blood and water gushing out onto the ground!

The Feast of Unleavened Bread lasts for seven days. The first day was a High Sabbath, and the last day was a High Sabbath, Exodus 12:16.

The next Holy Day was **FIRST FRUITS**. Yom Ha-Bikkurim). This was done the first day of the week following the weekly Sabbath. We know this because of Christ offering himself to His Father (John 20:17), the day after the weekly Sabbath. Therefore, it could be done any day during the week of Unleavened Bread so long as it was done after the weekly Sabbath.

On this Feast of First Fruits, the priest had to take a handful of barley that he had cut from the field and "wave" it by holding it up toward heaven and "presenting" it to God, Leviticus 23:20-21. This was often called the "wave offering". When Christ was resurrected, He told Mary not to touch Him for had not yet ascended to the Father, as I said above. He said this because He had to present Himself to the Father as the "First Fruits." "Christ has risen from the dead and become the First fruits, of those that sleep," 1 Corinthians 15:20-23. These passages also say, "Every man in his order; Christ the First Fruits and afterward they that are Christ's *at His coming*."

Next, is the **FEAST OF WEEKS**, which was later called in Greek, **PENTECOST** (Shavuot in Hebrew). Pentecost means fifty, because after the Feast of Unleavened Bread and First Fruits, seven weeks were counted and then one day added, thus fifty, Leviticus 23:16-17.

This was the festival where the Holy Spirit, "the Comforter", came, John 14:16. It was the Holy Day the Lord told them to wait for at Jerusalem, Acts 2:1-21. This day was when the "first harvest" began. Acts 2:41, says that three-thousand were added to the body of Christ that day. This is an ongoing feast, as everyday there are more being added to the fold. If the first Christians had not kept this feast, a Holy Day of God, none of this would have been fulfilled.

Now, these are the spring feasts. God's calendar begins the New Year at about the spring equinox. The first month on God's calendar is called Abib, Aviv or Nisan. God's number, however, for "completeness" is **seven** and the three final Holy Days or "latter Holy Days" begins in the seventh month.

Moses was instructed that this next Holy Day unto the Lord was to be done on the *first day* of the **seventh** month, Leviticus 23:24. The seventh month is Tishri. It is not July, for July is a "Roman month" on a "Roman calendar". God's seventh month begins around what we know as late September. This Holy Day is the fifth and is the **FEAST OF TRUMPETS (Yom Teruah** in Hebrew, which means "Day of Blowing"). This festival represents a day in God's plan that has *not yet happened.* On this day, trumpets (*shofars,* rams' horns) were **blown** and this day has **not yet come to pass.** Just like the ones before it, it will be fulfilled. Christians all over the world will be waiting for this day, because this day represents the day that the **"Trumpet,"** (the seventh or last, 1 Corinthians 15:52) will sound that will *wake the dead* at the **resurrection!** This is also in Matthew 24:31 and Revelation 11:15.

On the *tenth day* of the seventh month, is another Holy Day, the sixth, and it is the **DAY OF ATONEMENT,** Leviticus 23:27 (**Yom Kippur** in Hebrew). Atonement means "at one" with God. After we are resurrected, we are gathered to meet the Lord in the air and we are forever with Him from that point on.

Now, where do we go from there? The next festival tells us. Exodus 23: 16, "and the *feast of ingathering*, which is at the end of the year, when you have gathered in your crops out of the field."
Leviticus 23:42, "You shall dwell in booths seven days; all that are Israelites born shall *dwell in booths*."
Yes, this is the **FEAST OF INGATHERING or FEAST OF TABERNACLES** and is the seventh Holy Day. Tabernacle means to "dwell" or live with. This festival is also called the **Festival of Booths** (Sukkot in Hebrew). Sukkah means booth or hut. This festival is sometimes referred to as Hosannah Rabah, which means "Oh great day of Salvation." This Holy Day is mentioned in Exodus 23:16 and 34:22. It is explained in Leviticus 23:42. On the

fifteenth day of the seventh month, the Israelites were instructed to make *"temporary"* booths or structures and to dwell in them for the week of this festival. They had to go to Jerusalem each year and do this (if they were close enough). This festival represents God's "ingathering" or "fall harvest" of His people as described by the parable in Matthew 13:39. This is very clear, for Christ Himself says, "The harvest is the end of the world and the reapers are the angels." This festival represents the time (right after the resurrection) that **His saints are taken to Jerusalem** to live and reign with Him **one thousand years** on this earth, Jude 14 and Revelation 5:10. Living in Jerusalem is only *temporary*, however, because after the thousand years are over, He makes a new heaven and new earth and we will live with Him forever, Revelation 21:1.

Furthermore, there is one other Holy Day, but *it is attached* to the Feast of Tabernacles. At the end of the seven days of Tabernacles is the **GREAT DAY** or **Eighth Day**, Leviticus 23:36. It is called **Yom Atzarah** in Hebrew, which means "Day of Assembly." On this day, there was to be an "offering made by fire". This day represents the "day of assembly" of all those that have ever lived. It will be at the **Great White Throne Judgment**, which is at the end of the thousand-year reign of Christ on earth. It is also when the Devil and his angels along with the wicked are thrown into the "lake of fire", Revelation 19:20 to 20:15.

In the Bible, the eighth day also represents a **new beginning.** This will be the time when each person that enters His Kingdom will be given a "white stone" (Revelation 2:17) with his new name on it. When a male child was born, he was circumcised on the *eighth day* and given a name. This "eighth day" is a picture of the eighth thousand-year day of God (a thousand years is as one day with God, Psalm 90:4 and 2 Peter 3:8). God has given the human race a six-thousand-year period to do as he wishes. God will have to intervene at the end of this time or man will destroy himself off the face of the earth, Matthew 24:22. During this time, God has been bringing about His plan of salvation and redemption. Then on the seventh thousand-year period (the millennium), God, along with man, will rest and the world will be at peace. The beginning of the eighth thousand-year period, is when we begin anew with a new heaven and new earth and the final enemy (death) has been destroyed, 1 Corinthians 15:26 and Revelation 21:4.

When a faithful Jewish person accepts Christ as their Messiah, they need not change anything, for they are already keeping God's Holy Days and His Commandments. Christ and His disciples were Jews as were most of the first Christians. When we Christians see things through their eyes, we get a new and true perspective of the Scriptures and a much better understanding of what the Lord said and meant for all of His followers to do.

I have a new book titled "God's Holy Days". It goes into more detail about them and what they mean.

Chapter 8

What Day is the Sabbath?

This is easy. In Genesis 2:2-3, it says that God rested on the "seventh" day. He sanctified it or "set it apart" as a Holy Day. This is what holy means; it means to be set apart. This was not a day for "Jews." The Jews would not be on earth for over two thousand years. It was for all of humanity. Later, when He had chosen Israel, He gave the "Ten Commandments" to Moses who gave them to His chosen nation. He had to choose a nation and the nation He chose was Israel. Then He had to choose a tribe, which was Judah. King David was chosen out of that tribe, and then David's descendants to bring about the Messiah. That is why Christ was sometimes called the Son of David.

The Sabbath was and is the seventh day of the week. God has not changed and He did not change the weekly Sabbath, Malachi 3:6. The first Christians kept this day as the Sabbath for over three hundred years and it is easy to see in the book of Acts. They also kept all of God's Holy Days. If you read any authoritative book about how things were changed, you will find that Constantine changed the months and God's Holy Days when he instituted "Christianity" around 325 A.D. for the Roman Empire. The Ten Commandments says to "keep the Sabbath" holy or set apart. Remember what the Lord said to the rich young ruler in Matthew 19:17; "Keep the Commandments" if you want eternal life.

Some say that because Christ rose from the dead on Sunday morning, things changed. This is **a lie**! Here another mystery, He did not rise on Sunday morning! He had already risen when the women came to the tomb. If you know God's Holy Days, you know how God told the people (His chosen people) to keep them and then you will understand this. The Lord came into Jerusalem on the donkey on the Sabbath (Saturday), for "He is Lord of the Sabbath," Matthew 12:8. This was also a picture of the Jews bringing in the "Passover Lamb" into their homes, four days before it was to be killed. He cleared the moneychangers out of *His House* as the fathers of the people were taking the *leaven* out of their homes. He conducted the Passover meal after dark on what would be our **Tuesday night** (the day of Passover began at sunset, not at midnight like our days now begin). He died the next day during Passover as God's sacrifice on our **Wednesday**. He was laid in the ground that same day before sunset and He awoke 72 hours later, which was around sunset on Saturday! He said He would be in the heart of the earth for **"three days and three nights;"** the "sign of Jonah," Matthew 12:40. The angel came sometime during the night and opened the tomb before Sunday morning, Matthew 28:2. Therefore, Christ was resurrected and gone before Sunday morning even dawned! This means, His resurrection has nothing to do with God's Sabbath changing from Saturday to Sunday.

This is why the women had to wait until Sunday morning, "the first day of the week," to go to the tomb. They had prepared the spices that Friday, the only day they could have bought them. The day before, which was a Thursday, was a **High Sabbath of the Feast of Unleavened Bread**. You must remember the days of the week did not have the names they do today. Therefore, the weekly **Sabbath is Saturday,** from Friday evening at sunset, until Saturday evening at sunset.

Some use the passage in Acts 20:7, about the disciples meeting and breaking bread on the first day of the week. This only tells you that they met to eat. It also shows that if they met on the first day of the week, then the day before was the seventh day of the week, which was and is the Sabbath.

In Acts, Apostle Paul met many Sabbaths with Greeks and Jews at the synagogues to teach them; sometimes nearly everyone in town came to hear Paul speak, Acts 13:44. The early Christians were both Jews and Greeks. Below are several passages showing that Jews and Gentiles were coming to the synagogues on the Sabbath and hearing the Word of God being preached. The following Scriptures will prove that the early Christians met and worshiped on the Sabbath, the seventh day of the week, Saturday.

Acts 13:14 ". . . and they went into the synagogue on the Sabbath day . . ."

Acts 13:27 ". . . the voices of the prophets, which are read every Sabbath day. . ."

Acts 13:42 ". . . the Gentiles asked that these words might be preached to them the next
Sabbath."

Acts 13:44 ". . . the next Sabbath day almost the entire city came together to hear the
Word of God"

Acts 15:21 ". . . it being read in the synagogues every Sabbath day."

Acts 16:13 ". . . on the Sabbath we went out of the city by a riverside, where prayer was
made.

Acts 17:2 ". . . Paul, as his manner was, went in unto them and for three Sabbath days
reasoned with them out of the Scripture."

Acts 18:4 ". . . he reasoned in the synagogue every Sabbath and persuaded the Jews and
Greeks."

If the Lord would have changed something, I am sure He would have told us. In fact, he said the opposite. He said,

"I did not come to change the law, but to fulfill it,"
Matthew 5:17.

Chapter 9

When was Christ Born?

If you keep God's Holy Days, you will also keep
Christ's conception, His birth, His death and His return. As I
said, these days do not come on the same day each year.
That is one reason the Bible does not tell us what day Christ
was born. If people kept that day, they would not keep
God's Holy Days. If, however, they keep His Holy days,
they will see a picture of His birth, death, resurrection, the
sending of the Holy Spirit, His return and our resurrection.
They would also see a picture of His reign on earth for one
thousand years and the Judgment Day.

The Bible tells us that John the Baptist was conceived
six months before Christ, Luke 1:26. That means He was
born almost exactly six months later than John was. John's
father, a priest named Zachariah, was serving in the temple
at Jerusalem when the angel of the Lord appeared to him
and told him he was to have a son, Luke 1:13. He served
"according to his course," Luke 1:8. Lots were cast to
determine which family of men were to serve and what time
that service was to be done. Zachariah was of "the course of
Abia," Luke 1:8. Many would only get to serve once in their
lifetime because there were so many in line to do so. As
soon as Zachariah was finished at the temple, he went home
to his wife, Elizabeth, and she conceived John.

Six months after the angel had appeared to Zachariah;
the angel appeared to Mary and told her she was to have a
son by the Holy Spirit, Luke 1:28-38. She was also told to

call His name Yeshua (Jesus as most know it). Yeshua means Salvation.

When was this? Most likely it was on **"The Feast of Dedication"** which would later be called Hanukkah. This is the festival of **"lights"** and He was "the Light" of the world, John 8:12 and 9:5. This makes perfect sense. He was defiantly not born in December, because the shepherds in Luke 2:8 were with their sheep and they always brought them down from the mountains and hills and put them in pens during the winter months. It was hundreds of years later, that the "Roman Church" changed God's days (or tried to change them) and said He was born at the same time that the pagans celebrated the winter solstice. This was prophesied in Daniel 7:25 that the "Fourth Empire" (the Roman Empire) would "think to change times and laws."

If He died on Passover (one of God's Holy Days) and was the First Fruits (one of God's Holy Days), it makes perfect sense that He was conceived on a very important day. If He was conceived on Hanukkah, then nine months later, He would be born at the beginning of the Feast of Tabernacles. Tabernacle means to "dwell with" and He came to earth to dwell with us. "The Word was made flesh and *dwelt* among us," John 1:14. Eight days after He was born, was also a High Sabbath on which He was circumcised and given the name, Yeshua. He also should return on a Holy Day, or very near it. I will talk about this later.

Chapter 10

Who was John the Baptist?

John was the "One crying in the wilderness" to prepare the way of the Lord, Matthew 3:3, Mark 1:3, Luke 3:4 and John 1:23. The last book of the "Old Testament" Malachi 4:5 says, "I will send you Elijah the prophet before the **Great and Dreadful Day of the Lord.**"

This is why the Jews (as a whole) did not recognize John and who or what he was. He came in the "spirit of Elijah," Matthew 11:14 and Mark 9:12. If you read about the Prophet Elijah, he had power to call fire down from heaven and do all kinds of miracles. He also warned his nation to repent and turn to God.

John did not do miracles, stop the rain, or cause fire to come down from heaven like Elijah, but many of John's messages were not for that time, but when "the Great and Dreadful Day of the Lord" would come, which is still in the future. John's message is exactly what the "Two Witnesses" at the end of time will be preaching, except this time they *will* have the power that the Prophet Elijah did to stop the rain and "strike the earth with all manner of plagues," Revelation 11:6.

Christ did not come with fire and judgment the first time; He came as a lamb led to the slaughter, Isaiah 53:7 and Acts 8:32. However, when He comes to earth the second time, He will come just as John the Baptist said. If you read the book of Revelation you will read about the **Day of the Lord** and this was what John preached.

Chapter 11

Are Angels Real?

Angels are messengers of God. Psalms 104:4, "God makes His angels spirits, His messengers a flaming fire." They were created even before the universe began. This is told in Job 38:7. When the stars were created the "sons of God" shouted for joy.

Angels are mentioned about three-hundred times in the Bible. There are billions of them. There has to be to carry out all the work they do. "The angel of the Lord encamps round about those that fear him and will deliver them," Psalm 34:7. It was angels that announced the birth of Christ. It was angels that appeared to many people in the Bible to give them a message from God or to carry out a job they were sent to do. In 2 Kings 19:35 an angel killed 85,000 men of the Assyrian army while they slept one night.

It was an angel that appeared to Manoah, Samson's father and his mother before Samson was born and told them they were to have a son. The angel would not reveal his name when asked because he said it was a secret. The wife of Manoah said that the angel's face looked "very terrible" or frightening and she knew it was an angel of God, Judges 13:2-21. Then when Manoah built a fire on an altar unto God and angel's work was finished "the angel of the Lord ascended in the flame of the altar!" Now that is an exit!

There are several ranks of angels also. The Bible has revealed only a few and told their names. Michael and Gabriel are archangels. Lucifer was once a great archangel,

Isaiah 14:12, but sinned and now is "the adversary" or Satan.

Genesis 28:12 tells the story of Jacob's dream of a "ladder" where angels were ascending and descending between heaven and earth. This sounds like it was a vision showing Jacob that there are certain places (portals or doors) on earth where spirit beings can come and go.

The Bible says that Satan caused a third of the angels to rebel and be cast to earth, Revelation 12:4. Other angels committed an even more grievous sin before Noah's flood, Genesis 6:2. When these angels saw how beautiful some of the young women were, they changed themselves into human form and took the women as wives. They had children by these women and the offspring became great men, Genesis 6:4 and Jude 6.

After the flood, God took these "fallen angels" and put them into prison where they will be held until Judgment Day, 2 Peter 2:4. This judgment is also mentioned in 1 Corinthians 6:3, "Don't you know that we shall judge angels?"

Other "fallen angels" were "grounded". They are confined to the earth and must stay here until Judgment Day. These are what the Bible calls demons. They are spirits, but they have no form and must use humans to make their personality known. Some believe these had to be the human-angel hybrids. The flood would have killed their body but the "spirit half would have lived. This is very possible because Christ said they had to go into a person or they would wander the earth, which terrified them. Matthew 8:32 shows how frightened these demons became when Christ met them. These evil spirits begged Christ to let them go into a herd of hogs because they knew He had the power to punish them right then or put them in prison until Judgment Day, Matthew 8:29.

Some of the more powerful fallen angels or demons influence people to do evil and we must fight against them

(Ephesians 6:11-12). Many do not realize that Satan has great power and is "the god of this world" and "the prince of the power of the air," 1 Corinthians 4:4 and Ephesians 2:2. Some of the fallen angels have very great power, Revelation 9:14. Four "angels" (demons) will be responsible for killing one third of humanity in an eleven-month period! These are "fallen angels that have been "bound" or put in prison until the end of time. Then just before the battle at Armageddon, they will be let out to cause havoc on the earth. In Revelation 16:13, three other **"evil spirits working miracles"** cause the kings of the earth to come to Armageddon to battle the Lord at His return and will try to destroy God's city, Jerusalem.

In the book of Job (Job 1:6 and 2:1), Satan presented himself before God when there was a gathering of "the sons of God". These meetings must be mandatory just as God had all the men of Israel present themselves three times a year before Him, Deuteronomy 16:16. Therefore, God must have certain times that all the angels must appear before Him in heaven.

During one of these times in heaven, when Satan presented himself before the Lord, he acquired permission to test Job.

One thing Satan was able to do was to cause a tornado to come and kill Job's children. Many times, what people think is an "act of God" may very well be an act of "the god of this world", 2 Corinthians 4:4. The name Satan in Hebrew is Hasatan, which means "the adversary".

There is a story in the gospel of Luke 13:11 of an elderly woman that had been bent over to where she could barely walk and could not straighten herself up. In verse 16, Christ said that Satan had bound her with this deformity for the past eighteen years. In Luke 22:31 Christ said that Satan had wanted to have Peter to try to make his faith fail. Christ prayed that this would not happen.

Many also think that Satan is already in hell, but this is not the truth. Satan is still in heaven! Revelation 12: 10 says that he is "before our God day and night accusing God's people." This passage is just before there is war in heaven and Satan is kicked out. When he is cast to earth, he is full of wrath and knows he has but a short time before God intervenes in human affairs and puts him in prison for a thousand years. Therefore, he is full of anger and tries to destroy all of God's followers. Most know this three-and-a-half-year period of "Satan's wrath" as the Great Tribulation. I will speak more about this in another chapter.

God calls angels "sons of God" in the book of Job, but He also calls men sons of God, Isaiah 41:23, Psalm 82:6 and John 10:34-35. It is very likely that there are many other "beings" in the vast universe that God thinks of as His sons.

We will be very surprised when we see what angels look like. Isaiah 14:16 says that when God restrains Satan at the end of this age, people will look at him, be shocked and say, "Is this the man that made the earth to tremble, that shook the kingdoms?"

Angels continue to travel back and forth from heaven and earth. They also must be able to travel to many other places. When Satan appeared before God in the book of Job, God asked him where he had been. Satan replied that he had been going back and forth in the earth. By giving that answer, it appears there are many other planets where he could have been.

God also says that the earth is His "footstool." If our planet is His footstool, then what are His other more important planets? He says in Isaiah 40:15 that the nations of the earth are as a drop in a bucket, as the small dust on a scale. In verse 17 He says that "All the nations before Him are as nothing and are counted to Him less than nothing and vanity." Therefore, what are His important places? If our planet is as a speck of dust on a scale and does not matter, then where are His planets or places that *are* very important? It is true that if you look at the universe, even our sun is only a speck of light on one of the spirals of one galaxy of the billions of galaxies. Therefore, in that respect, our planet is as nothing. However, the Creator of the universe loved His creation so much that He came to this speck of dust and died for us!

Now back to angels. The reason there are fallen angels is that they rebelled against God. We do not know everything they did, but we do know Satan was and is their leader.

One thing some of the rebellious angels did was to leave "their habitation" which means where they lived, came to earth and fathered children. I also believe that these "offspring" between angels and human women are the ones that built some of the marvels of the ancient world. Stone Hinge is one example. In addition, in the high mountains of Machu Picchu, Peru, South America, there are stones weighing several hundred tons that have been moved 8,000 feet up the mountain. Not only have they been moved up the steep mountain, but they were stacked together and cut with many angles so they fit together perfectly. Here they have been for centuries. People that did not have a written language nor had even invented the wheel supposedly did this! Even today, with all our heavy machinery and computers we cannot do what these "primitive people" did. These places would not have been destroyed by a flood. Moreover, centuries later, people coming upon these mysterious ruins would believe that "gods" made them. Besides that, early civilizations would have most certainly dwelt there believing the gods should be worshiped that had built such wonders.

Also, in Peru, there are depictions, called Nazca Lines, of animals. They are on the flat tops of mountains, are hundreds of feet long, and can only be recognized as pictures by being seen from high in the air. Why are they here? You would have to fly in order to recognize what they are. One depiction is of a spider. This species of spider has only recently been discovered. The depiction of this very tiny spider also shows its sex organ. The strange thing about this, is that the sex organ is microscopic and cannot been seen with the naked eye! So how did people know what the sex organ looked like if they never saw it?

Also, in Peru, there have been some very strange stones discovered; thousands of them. They are called the "Inca Stones" and they have etched pictures on them of dinosaurs! Several of the species of dinosaurs are recognizable and some have never been seen. One species depicted on a stone shows a textured skin. Only recently has fossil remains of the skin of this dinosaur been found, and amazingly it shows that it indeed had textured skin. What is more astounding is that some of the pictures of dinosaurs also show humans with them!

Moreover, it has only recently been discovered that the brain capacity of some of these people were 25% larger than modern humans. According to the World Book Encyclopedia 1990 edition, the belief of the Incas is that their "brothers and sisters" were "sent to earth" by their "father the sun" to teach and rule the people!

Jude 6, says that some of the pre-flood angels left their "first estate" (rank or position) and left their own "habitation" (place where they lived or dwelt) and came to earth. Here they fathered children Genesis 6:4. These children died in the flood, but their fathers were angelic beings in human form and did not die, but were cast into prison until Judgment Day, Jude 6.

This "great sin" of having children by a human woman is most likely what happened in the Garden of Eden, which I discus in the chapter "What Really Happened in the Garden of Eden?"

Just as God uses people to carry out His work on earth, He uses these spirit beings called angels, to carry out His work between heaven and earth. In Matthew 18:10 the Lord said to be careful not to offend God's children because they have angels assigned to them that see and come before God in heaven.

Hebrews 13:2 says, "Some have entertained angels and knew it not." We never know when we meet a stranger if it is really a person or an angel. If it were an angel, they would most likely come at a time in your life when you are in desperate need. You would never see this "person" again, so there would be no way you could know if it was an angel or not. In the story of Balaam in Numbers 22:23, Balaam's donkey could see an angel that was standing before them with a sword, but Balaam could not. It could be possible then that all animals can see spirit beings. Many birds see in ultraviolet light. When Christ spoke to Nicodemus, He said that a spirit is like the wind. You can see its effects, yet you can't see it, John 3:8. Angels must therefore be in a different dimension than we are. In their dimension, they can interact with us but we are unable to see them unless they choose to cross over into our dimension or if God "opens our eyes" in order for us to see them. Christ could see them because on several occasions He spoke to demons.

In the resurrection, the Lord will send out His angels to gather His people, Matthew 24:31. How many angels will be assigned to each person? There will be at least two. I myself have always believed that there will be two (one for each arm). How do we know this? In the parable of Lazarus and the rich man (Luke 16:22), Lazarus was "carried by angels into Abraham's bosom." It did not say an angel, but angels, so there had to be two or more.

When we come out of the grave with a new resurrected body, the angels will have to be there to wrap clothes around us as we come up. This coming out of "mother earth" will be the time we are "born again." I explain this in the chapter "What does it mean to be Born Again?"

Yes, angels are very real and they are all around us. They are invisible to us now, but someday we will be like them and we will be able to see them and communicate with them directly.

In 2 Kings 6:17, Elisha's servant sees a mountain full of God's fiery chariots and horses when his "eyes are opened."

Today, science is just beginning to understand some of the things that the Bible alludes to, such as other dimensions. Heaven and God's throne may not be that far away. It says in 2 Samuel 22:10 and Psalm 18:11 that God bowed the heavens and came down and darkness was under His feet. In Psalm 18:11 "He made darkness His secret hiding place." Is it possible that "dark matter" that many scientists say covers more of the universe than visible matter, is where God has His throne and His dwelling place? Could this be the dimension that all spirit beings live in?

I believe it was no accident that it was very dark and with thick clouds the day the Lord was dying on the cross. Is it possible that this was because there were spacecraft hovering with thousands of angels watching? I reveal what the Bible says about how angels travel and how Christ will return in the chapter, "When is Christ returning?"

Chapter 12

The Time of the End

In Daniel 12:4 it says, *"But you, O Daniel shut up the words and seal the book, even unto the time of the end; many shall run to and fro, and knowledge shall be increased."*

This passage tells us, that near the end of time, humans will be traveling rapidly all over the world and knowledge will be at an unprecedented high. This describes perfectly our world today.

Since I was fourteen-years-old, I began studying the prophecies in the Bible about the Lord's return. Over the years, I have seen many of the events foretold in the Bible come to reality.

One mystery that was made clear and could not be understood until just recently is the prophecy of the two witnesses dying in the streets of Jerusalem. It says in Revelation 11:8-10 that God's two witnesses will be killed and will lie in the street for three and a half days and will not be buried. It also says that the people of the earth will see their dead bodies and shall rejoice and be happy and will send gifts to one another because these two men were hated. This was not possible until we had satellite communications. The Bible says all that dwell on the earth will see them, declare a "holiday" and send gifts to one another. This prophecy was written when the fastest means of transportation was by horseback. It would have taken months just to spread the word to a few nearby countries, let alone the entire earth, which was not even known then. I discuss this further in a chapter on the two witnesses, who they are and where they are.

There are many other prophecies that could not take place until modern times. Everything that is to happen is in God's control. He has *a set time* for things to unfold and take place, Job 14:13 and Psalm 102:13.

Today you hear many people talking about Armageddon and natural disasters with "Biblical proportions." There are movies about the "end of time" and there are even popular movies about the "rapture" but most do not understand the truth. In the following chapters, I will quote many Scriptures about what will happen at the "time of the end" and how these events will unfold. The answers are in your Bible and have been for centuries, only today, however, are many of these Scriptures understandable.

I have more in the next chapters and I have also written other books on this subject. They are: *The Coming Invasion, Death is His Name, A Rude Awakening* and *Mystery of the Millennium.*

Chapter 13

What is the "Mark of the Beast"?

There is so much confusion about this subject and many "theories" about what it is. The Bible tells us about it, but leaves much not revealed. This is on purpose, because it is meant to give you a heads up, so that when it takes place you will know. The wicked will not know or care, because the Scriptures were written for God's people.

In 2 Thessalonians chapter 2, much is said about the Antichrist and the coming of the Lord. I have already spoken of this earlier but it bears repeating. In 2 Thessalonians 2:11 it says that because of people not wanting to know the truth and because they love unrighteousness, God will send *"strong delusion"* so they might believe a lie. In verse 12, it says God sends this delusion so *"they might be damned."*

This is talking about when the Antichrist comes on the scene. He is also called *"the Man of Sin"*; the *"Son of Perdition"; "That Wicked One"* and *"The Beast."*

The book of 2 Thessalonians is about the coming of the Lord and verse 1 begins with these words, *"Now we beseech you brothers about the coming of the Lord and our gathering together unto Him."*

This is very clear. This is speaking about Christ returning to earth, the resurrection of the dead and the changing of "we who are alive and remain" being "caught up." Most believe this is called "the rapture."

In order to understand how and why the resurrection, not "rapture", will take place, you must first understand what happens when you die. Many, if not most, Christians haven't been told the truth and this is the very reason there is misinformation about what people call "the rapture."

In the next verse of 2 Thessalonians that I was quoting, Apostle Paul says that he does not want the Thessalonians to be "shaken in mind or troubled" because there were rumors that the Day of Christ was at hand. *Day of Christ* is also the same as *Day of the Lord*, the end of time, the coming of Christ and the resurrection.

This is going on today. Preachers all the time are saying, "The Lord could come at any moment and 'catch away' His church. Paul said this *"is a lie!"*

Paul makes it clear that *Christ cannot return* to earth to resurrect His people and gather "we that are alive and remain" yet. He goes on to say in verse 3, "Let no man deceive you by any means; for that day will not come *except* there comes a **'falling away first'** and that **'Man of Sin** the 'Son of Perdition' (the Antichrist) **be revealed**." This is crystal clear. Christ cannot come back to get His people until two things happen.

The falling away is mentioned in Revelation 1:20 to chapter 3:22. Here God is speaking to the seven churches. These seven churches represent seven consecutive states His church will be in over the course of the centuries and at the time of His return. The "last state" the church will be in is a "lukewarm state". The church, by this time, has strayed so far away from the truth and has let sin come in so much that they have "fallen away" from God. This is happening right now. Many, if not most, that call themselves Christians have lost their way. They are like the proverbial frog that sits in hot water and does not know the water is getting hotter until it is too late and it dies. They often cannot tell what is right or wrong. Little by little, the moral fiber of the country, the world and the minds of the people has been slowly eroded away. They see nothing wrong with what God has said is a sin or even an abomination to Him. The wicked have slowly turned their (the Christians as well as the unbelievers) minds and hearts away from God and replaced it with a "new morality". People today are becoming desensitized to sin; it will only get worse. The Bible says in Proverbs 14:12-13 "There is a way which seems right unto a man, but the end thereof are the ways of death."

This was also prophesied to happen. In Isaiah 3:9 it says, "The show of their countenance (or expression on their faces) does witness against them; and they declare *their sin as Sodom*, they hide it not. Woe unto their soul! For they have rewarded evil unto themselves."

Today, God has already begun to separate the sheep from the goats. How do we know He is doing this? Because in Romans 1:18-32 it says, "For the wrath of God is revealed from heaven against all ungodliness and unrighteousness of men, who hold the truth in unrighteousness; Because that which may be known of God is manifest in them; for God hath showed it unto them. For the invisible things of Him from the creation of the world are clearly seen, being understood by the things that are made, even his eternal power and Godhead, so that they are without excuse. Because that, when they knew God, they glorified him not as God, neither were thankful; but became vain in their imaginations, and their foolish heart was darkened. Professing themselves to be wise, they became fools. And changed the glory of the incorruptible God into an image made like to corruptible man, and to birds, and four-footed beasts, and creeping things. Wherefore *God also gave them up* to uncleanness through the lusts of their own hearts, to *dishonor their own bodies between themselves*; who changed the truth of God into a lie, and worshipped and served the creature more than the Creator, who is blessed forever. Amen.

"For this cause, God gave them up unto *vile affections*: for even their women did change the *natural use into that which is against nature*. And likewise, also the men, *leaving the natural use of the woman*, burned in their lust one toward another; *men with men working that which is unseemly,* and receiving in themselves that recompense of their error which was meet. And even as they did not like to retain God in their knowledge, **God gave them over to a reprobate mind**, to do those things which are not convenient; being filled with all unrighteousness, fornication, wickedness, covetousness, maliciousness; full of envy, murder, debate, deceit, malignity; whisperers, backbiters, haters of God, despiteful, proud, boasters, inventors of evil things, disobedient to parents. Without understanding, covenant breakers, without natural affection, implacable, unmerciful: Who knowing the judgment of God, that they which commit such things are worthy of death, not only do the same, *but have pleasure in them that do them."* KJV

In my book, *Evolution: The Big Lie!* I use part of this passage to show that many have pushed God out of their lives and do not believe in Him but have faith that the world came about by chance and coincidence.

At the end of the age, just before the Lord returns, believers will be complacent and think they are fine. They, however, will be blind. Because of their unbelief and love of the things in this world, God will wake them up. God says that because He loves His people, He will chastise them, Revelation 3:19. This "Laodicean church" thinks it is rich, has many material things and is in need of nothing. God, however, thinks differently. He tells them that they are poor, blind, miserable and naked! In addition, because they think that they are rich, He challenges them to buy Him gold "tried in the fire", Revelation 3:18. What does this mean? Gold is purified by "going through fire." When gold ore is put into a kiln (an oven or furnace heated by a very hot fire), all the "impurities come to the surface". What is left is pure gold. God is saying that because they think they are okay, but cannot see their own sin, He will take them "through the fire of tribulation." He is speaking of the Great Tribulation at the end of this age, just before He returns. This way, they will be purified, when their sins come to the surface, where they can be seen and "skimmed off."

After *His church* goes through the Great Tribulation, He says they will not be naked but will be clothed with white raiment and their eyes will be healed with eye salve so they can see, (see the truth).

The Bible also says Revelation 18:4-5 "And I heard another voice from heaven, saying, 'Come out of *her*, My people, that you be not partakers of *her* sins, and that you receive not of *her* plagues.'" This shows that God will "draw" His people out from among the false teachings of "her" the "woman in red" that sits on the Beast, Revelation 18:4, which I discuss in the next chapter.

Many today, especially in the western world, think that since they are Christians they will not have to go through The Tribulation. They believe the Lord will "catch them away" in a "secret rapture". If you read carefully in Revelation 12:17 it says that Satan will make war with "the remnant of her seed (the "Woman's seed", which are Christians), that *keep the Commandments of God* and have the testimony of Yeshua (Jesus Christ). These are Christians that "keep the Commandments". Most "Christians" today do not even believe they have to keep them. Many do not even know what they are. They don't even know what day the Sabbath is! These "lukewarm Christians" believe that they are better than the Apostles and the early Christians that were killed for their faith. These are the very ones God will require to go through The Tribulation to purify them!

Now the "church of Philadelphia" will also be here at the same time. God says in Revelation 3:10, "That because you have kept the word of my patience, I will keep you from the 'hour of temptation' that shall come upon all the world, to try them that dwell upon the earth."

This church is the "woman" in Revelation 12:6 that is "given wings of an eagle" and "flees into the wilderness where she is nourished for three and a half years," verse 14. This "hour of temptation" mentioned above and this three-and-a-half-year period is the time of The Great Tribulation.

A few Christians will be protected during The Great Tribulation. They will not, however, be taken to heaven. The Bible says they will be taken to a place of safety *somewhere on earth* that God has prepared. Luke 21:36 says to "Pray always that you *are worthy* to escape all these things."

Now that we understand this, we can begin to understand what the "mark of the Beast" is.

Revelation 13:1-8 speaks about a "beast". In verse16, it says that this "Beast" will make everyone receive a "mark". The mark will either be on the right hand or on the forehead.

You must go to Daniel 7:7-23 to understand what this "Beast" is. Verse 23 says that this Beast is the "fourth kingdom" that will come upon the earth. I explain in the next chapter, that the Great Image and the four beasts represent the same empires that were to come, starting with the Babylonian Empire. This last one was to be the Roman Empire.

Now we know what the Beast is. The Roman Empire was here when Christ first came and it will be here when He returns. Revelation 1:7 says, "Behold He comes with clouds and ever eye shall see Him, and **they** also **which pierced Him**. It was Romans that nailed Him to the cross and the Bible says that Romans will see Him coming.

The Roman Empire has been revived six times according to history. The Bible says that it will live seven times, thus the seven heads of the Beast. It has one more revival to take place.

The vision of the Great Image in the book of Daniel shows that at the end of time ten kings will join for "one hour" (a short time). During this time, the "Rock" from heaven (Christ), will come and destroy the entire image or system of the world, Daniel 2:34. After its destruction, God will set up His Kingdom on earth.

The Man of Sin is first mentioned in Daniel 8:9 and says that he grows very great and he takes away the daily sacrifice and makes the abomination of desolation.

The "mark" that the Beast forces people to take is a number. The number is 666. No one is sure what these numbers mean, but it will be clear when it happens. This number will the "signature" of the "Beast". Revelation 13:18 says, "The number of the beast is the number of a man." Therefore, the man and revived Roman Empire will most likely share this number. It could very well be that the Roman letters in his name will equal 666, when the value of the letters are added up. Whatever it is, God's people will know when it happens.

There is one more clue about "the mark". Many of the prophecies are duel in their meaning and fulfillment. The "mark" most likely has a duel meaning. It could be an actual "mark" or number and a symbolic "mark".

Those who follow God will be keeping his commandments, "Revelation 12:17. The commandment that distinguishes God's people from the rest of the world is keeping of the Sabbath, Exodus 31:13 & 17 and Ezekiel 20:12&20. God himself, at the creation of the world, instituted the Sabbath and it was also chosen as a sign between him and his people. Those that follow the Antichrist will not be keeping the Sabbath, which means the seventh day, but will be keeping the first day of the week (Sunday).

Further proof that this may very well mean the "mark" is because the "mark" is on the "forehead" or in the "right hand."

The forehead is our mind and the right hand is what we use to do our work. When the priests were anointed, God told Moses to have them anointed on their right ear, right thumb and right big toe, Leviticus 8:24, Exodus 29:20. The ear signifies what we hear, the hand signifies what we do, the toe signifies where we go and the forehead signifies what we think.

Exodus 13:15-16, "And it will be like a sign on your hand and a symbol on your forehead that the Lord brought us out of Egypt with his mighty hand."

When Christ was at the Last Supper, he told his disciples to, "Do this in remembrance of me." God led the Israelites out of the bondage and slavery of Egypt. Christ brought his people out of the bondage of sin and death. The first Passover was a rehearsal for the one Christ did at the Last Supper. The "blood of the Lamb" that was put on the doorpost in Egypt was the symbol of Christ's blood. The lamb's blood in Egypt saved any that believed from physical death. Christ blood saves any that believes from eternal death.

Those that will be following Christ during the time the Antichrist is here will have the "sign" the "mark" in their minds by observing the Sabbath. They will also have the sign on their hands by not working on the Sabbath. Those that have the "mark of the beast" will be working on the Sabbath and not observing it. The beast will try to force everyone to observe "his ways" not God's.

In Revelation 13:5, it says that this Beast was to continue for 42 months (three and a half years). The next verse, Revelation 13:6, says that he was given a mouth to speak blasphemies against God and heaven. It also says in Revelation 13:4 that Satan gives power to the Beast. The same Scripture also says, "Who is like the Beast? Who is able to make war with him?"

Revelation 13:7 then says that he made war with the saints (God's people) and power was given him over all races and nations (same as Revelation 12:17). This same event (the war against the saints), is prophesied in Daniel 7:21 and 25.

During this time, everyone will have to receive "his mark" or they cannot buy or sell, Revelation 13:16-17. Most on earth will willingly take the mark. They will care more about filling their bellies and having material things than following God and "being religious". If a person takes the mark, this means that they will be part of the revived Roman government. This Man of Sin, the Antichrist, will be the leader and he will be so powerful (and charismatic) that the world will follow him, Revelation 13:3.

How will he convince people to go along with him? This is not hard to understand. Besides being so charismatic, he will be very smart. Daniel 8:23 says, "In the latter time of their kingdom (Fourth Empire), a king (or leader) of fierce countenance and understanding dark sentences shall stand up." In Judges 13:6 a visitor comes to Samson's parents before he is born and it says, "his countenance was like that of an angel of God and very terrible." 2 Corinthians 11:14 says, "Do not marvel, for Satan himself is transformed into an angel of light."

The Antichrist will be so persuasive that people will follow him like sheep. He will use many words to trick people into believing he has the answers to the world's problems. He will bring peace to the Middle East. He will have "a plan" to bail out the world's economy.

One way he can do this is by giving every person on earth an international number. No one will have your personal number and it will not be on a card that can be stolen. The number will be "imprinted" onto a person's right hand. If they do not have a right hand or if it is crippled, deformed or injured, the number will be on their forehead. The number then can be scanned and all monetary transactions will be recorded. This way there will be no theft, no cheating on taxes, no buying of illegal items, such as drugs, guns, bomb making supplies, or other "contraband".

He will bring "peace" to the world and "by peace he shall destroy many", Daniel 8:25.

The Antichrist also has a partner. He is mentioned in Revelation 13:11. He is pictured as *a lamb*, but with horns and who speaks like a dragon. In Revelation 16:13 he is called "the false prophet." He will be a "religious leader" of the revived Roman Empire and will support what the Man of Sin is doing. He will persuade people to follow the Antichrist and he will cause people to worship the "Man of Sin" and do other things, even though it goes against Scripture.

One thing the "false prophet" will do is to force people to keep the first day of the week as the Sabbath (Sunday), instead of the seventh (Saturday), which is God's Sabbath and God's number. Satan's number is six. The false prophet and Man of Sin will also force people to keep "pagan holidays" and not allow them to keep God's Holy Days. "He will think to change times and seasons," which he already started doing three hundred years after Christ came the first time. Now, however, he will try to force all on earth to do what he wants, Daniel 7:25.

When this "Man of Sin" sits in the temple at Jerusalem (2 Thessalonians 2:4) and says that he is God, his true colors will be known and this is when he begins his "wrath" on God's people.

Satan has always wanted to be like God and to be worshiped. This will be his last chance to force people to worship him. Therefore, anyone that will not receive this mark and follow the Antichrist will be persecuted and, if possible, killed. This is when the great martyrdom takes place, Revelation 6:11. I have more on the abomination of desolation in the following chapter.

This is also the time that God's two witnesses will come on the scene to warn people not to take the mark.

Others also will know the truth and "shall instruct many", Daniel 11:33.

If you take the mark, it means that you will sell your soul. If you refuse to take it, you will be considered a "criminal" that wishes to break the "government's laws" and it will be open season on those that the "Beast" perceives as bad citizens.

After forty-two months, God will intervene and the world will finally see that they have been deceived by the "the woman dressed in red", which is the "false church" and they will turn on her, Revelation 17:16-18.

Chapter 14

When is Christ Returning?

After the Lord told His disciples about the temple's future destruction, they asked Him when it would happen and what would be the sign of His coming back to earth, Matthew 24, Luke 21 and Mark 13.

He gave them several signs to look for. One was the destruction of the temple in Jerusalem. This took place in A.D.70, and the Romans tore down every stone, just as Christ said would happen. Part of His prophecy was about the destruction of the temple and the armies surrounding Jerusalem in A.D. 70, but like many prophecies, it is "dual." There usually is a former and a latter fulfillment.

I hear preachers all the time taking things out of context and saying "these are signs." It is true, that there are many signs today, but when the "Day of the Lord" begins, there will be no mistaking it. Revelation 6:12-14: "When He had opened the sixth seal, and lo there was an earthquake; and the sun became black as sackcloth of hair and the moon became as blood; and the stars of heaven fell unto earth, even as a fig tree cast her unripe figs when she is shaken by a mighty wind. And heaven departed as a scroll when it is rolled together; and every mountain and island were moved out of their places." In verse 17, it says, "For **the great day of His wrath** has come and who will be able to stand?"

In Revelation 16:18: "There was a great earthquake such as was not since men were upon earth." In verse 20: "And every island fled away and the mountains were not found." How could this happen? Islands and every place on the globe are found by latitude and longitude. If the tectonic plates were to shift, the islands, mountains and even continents would be moved out of their places.

How could stars fall to earth? The "stars will fall to earth like a fig tree cast her untimely figs." What does this mean? It could be meteors falling, but He said the "stars" would fall. We say the sun rises and sets and so does the moon, but they appear to do so because the earth turns. In Isaiah 24:20, it says, "The earth shall reel to and fro like a drunkard and shall be removed like a cottage." If the earth is moving back and forth, it will look as if the stars are falling! In addition, it says that the sun and moon will not have any light, so it will be pitch black and the stars would be easily seen.

When I was young, I wondered how the sky could be rolled back like a scroll. If the clouds are rolled back to reveal Christ's coming there would be a tremendous noise, because the air masses would be breaking the sound barrier. It would be hundreds or thousands of times louder than jet planes breaking the sound barrier. We do not know if this rolling back like a scroll of the heavens will be worldwide or in a certain area over Jerusalem. I would think it would be worldwide for the Bible says, "Every eye shall see Him," Revelation 1:7. This also opens the possibility that came to me many years ago. Christ could be as large as He wishes to be, for He is a spirit. The Bible says, "He stretched forth the heaven as a curtain." He could stand before the earth and be so huge that every person on earth could see the anger in His eyes and the expression on His face. This may be why they will hide in the caves and "cry for the rocks and mountains to fall on them and hide them from **His face**," Revelation 6:15-16.

Some think the Lord returns and takes His people out before the tribulation or His wrath begins, but read the Scriptures. Revelation 7:3, "Hurt not the earth, neither the sea, nor the trees, till we have sealed the servants of our God in their foreheads." Then in verse 14, it says, "These are they, which came out of Great Tribulation."

"No man knows the day or hour" (Matthew 24:36) that He is returning, so these people that say He is coming on a certain day do not know. It does say, however, that you will know when it is near, even at the doors, Matthew 24:33 and Mark 13:29. He did give us signs, but I hear "preachers" all the time taking things out of context to "show" that He could come at any time. The Bible says He cannot come at any time. Just as He came the first time, there were certain prophesies which had to be fulfilled.

The book of **Daniel is the key** to the book **of Revelation**. The vision of the "**Great Image**," that God gave to Nebuchadnezzar, king of Babylon, and the vision that Daniel interpreted, tells what was to happen from that point in time until the Lord returns, Daniel 2:31-35.

This image had a head of **Gold**, which represented the Babylonian Empire. It had a chest and two arms of **Silver** that was to be the Medo-Persian Empire. Its belly was made of **Brass,** which was to be the Grecian Empire. Finally, the legs were of **Iron**, which was to be the Roman Empire. At the end of the feet, the toes were mixed with part iron and part miry clay.

The legs of this fourth empire are a clear representation of how the empire became split into two parts. The Roman Empire became so large that it could not govern itself, so it was divided into two seats of power; one at Rome and the other at Constantinople.

In addition, the Gold, Silver, Brass and Iron shows how each succeeding empire would be less glorious in beauty, but more powerful militarily in treading down those before it. This final empire was made of iron and iron "breaks in pieces" all before it, Daniel 7:23.

At the feet of this great image, this mixture of part iron and part miry clay means the empire will be made of many different nationalities of people. Just as clay and iron do not mix well and are partly strong and partly weak, they will not "cling" together for long, "an hour," which means a very short time as nations go. The toes represent ten kings or countries that will unite where the old Roman Empire once existed; and as it says in Daniel a "Stone" (Rock) will come from heaven and smash the feet of the Great Image and destroy it. Then this "Stone" (Christ and His Kingdom) will grow until it becomes a mountain that covers the entire world.

The "four beasts" in Daniel 7:3 are the same as the four empires of the image. The great image and the four beasts represent the "Babylonian system," which Christ will destroy when He returns.

In Revelation 17, "a woman", which represents "a church", rides or controls the Beast. This is a picture of the Revived Roman Empire. It is "The Beast that was, is not and yet is," Revelation 17:8. The woman that is riding and controlling the Beast is dressed in "scarlet" (Cardinal Red). She is the "false church" and she is destroyed along with the Beast, when Christ returns. Christ's church or "Bride" is dressed in "white" and is "without spot, wrinkle or blemish," Ephesians 5:27 and Revelation 21:2.

Out of this fourth empire (the Roman Empire) is to come the "Man of Sin" and the "False Prophet," and they will "think to change God's times and laws," Daniel 7:25. Therefore, the entire world has been deceived and will continue to be deceived until the two witnesses come and tell the truth. Even then, however, the world, as a whole, will not want to follow Christ or His teachings, but will want to continue to sin.

The Lord Himself said that the **key sign** of His return was the **Abomination of Desolation.** Matthew 24:15, "When you therefore shall see the abomination of desolation, spoken of by Daniel the prophet…"

If you read Matthew 24, Mark 13 and Luke 21, you get a brief outline of the signs of His coming. What He said in the Gospels is a brief synopsis of the "four horsemen of the apocalypse" in the book of Revelation.

Here is what he said in Matthew 24:3-13 "As he sat upon the Mount of Olives, the disciples came unto him privately, saying, 'Tell us, when shall these things be and what shall be the sign of thy coming and of the end of the world?'"

Yeshua (Jesus) answered and said unto them, "Take heed that no man deceives you. For many shall come in my name, saying, I am Christ; and shall deceive many. And you shall hear of wars and rumors of wars: see that you be not troubled: for all these things must come to pass, but the end is not yet. For nation shall rise against nation and kingdom against kingdom: and there shall be famines and pestilences and earthquakes, in different places. All these are the beginning of sorrows. Then shall they deliver you up to be afflicted and shall kill you: and ye shall be hated of all nations for my name's sake. And then shall many be offended and shall betray one another and shall hate one another. And many false prophets shall rise and shall deceive many. And because iniquity shall abound, the love of many shall wax cold. But he that shall endure unto the end, the same shall be saved."

Then down in verse 15, He says what sign there will be that sets all this in motion: "When ye therefore shall see *the abomination of desolation*, spoken of by *Daniel* the prophet, stand in the holy place, (whoso reads, let him understand). Verse 22 says, "For then shall be great tribulation, such as was not since the beginning of the world to this time, no, nor ever shall be. And except those days should be shortened, there should no flesh be saved: but for the elect's sake those days shall be shortened."

Christ then tells us that false prophets and evil people will try to trick Christians by saying that the Lord has come "secretly." Verse 23, "Then if *any man* shall say unto you, 'Lo, here is Christ, or there;' believe it not. Because there shall arise false Christs and false prophets and shall show great signs and wonders, insomuch that, if it were possible, they shall deceive the very elect. **Behold, I have told you before."**

Then He says, "Wherefore if they shall say unto you, 'Behold, He is in the desert' do not go forth: 'Behold, He is in the secret chambers,' believe it not. For as the lightning (sunshine) comes out of the east and shines even unto the west; so shall also the coming of the Son of man be."

He then tells us *specifically* *when* He is coming to get his people. "Immediately *after the tribulation* of those days shall the sun be darkened and the moon shall not give her light, and the stars shall fall from heaven, and the powers of the heavens shall be shaken. And then shall appear the sign of the Son of man in heaven: and then shall all the tribes of the earth mourn, and they shall see the Son of man coming in the clouds of heaven with power and great glory.

Now comes "the rapture" verse 31: "And he shall send his angels with a great sound of a trumpet, and they shall gather together his elect from the four winds, from one end of heaven to the other."

These first verses in Matthew 24 are listed the same as in the book of Revelation. **First**: the "false Christs" anti-Christ and the *white horseman*. **Second**: war and rumors of war, which is the *red horseman*. **Third**: are famines, the *black horseman*. **Fourth**: are disease epidemics, which is the *pale horse*.

The "fifth seal" in Revelation which is the "great martyrdom of Christians" at the end of time, is spoken of in Matthew 24:9. "Then shall they deliver you up to be afflicted and shall kill you: and you shall be hated of all nations for my name's sake."

As I said, the key to understanding the book of Revelation is the book of Daniel specifically the "abomination of desolation", which will be the trigger (or sign) that starts the "Great Tribulation." Most think that this

81

was fulfilled when Antiochus Epiphanes desecrated the temple, poured the blood of a pig on the altar (168 B.C.), and erected a statue of the god Zeus there. This was a "forerunner" or type of the Antichrist and Abomination of Desolation, which was to come later.

One other Scripture tells us that what Antiochus did may be a picture of what the Antichrist will do. Revelation 13:13-15 says that the Antichrist will make the people of the earth create an image of him. After they do, the Antichrist will "give life" to the image and cause it to speak." Once it speaks, it says that everyone on the earth should worship the "beast or be killed." Today there are "animated" robots that look exactly like famous people, such as Abraham Lincoln. They can move, speak and actually appear to be alive. Moreover, who knows how real they will appear in the future. If Antiochus erected a statue of Zeus in the temple, most likely the Antichrist will have his image there this time. Anyone coming into the temple would have bow down and worship him instead of God. I'm sure he would also make everyone on earth have small statues of himself so they could worship him at home or at work.

The Antichrist erecting a statue of himself in the new temple and saying that he is God is part of the abomination, but I believe there will be more. Now here are my thoughts about this: The **Abomination of Desolation** is going to be so terrible that there will be **war in heaven**! Revelation, chapter 12, says that Satan will be overthrown and driven from heaven along with his fallen angels. Many believe this has already happened, but if you read the Scriptures, it says that Satan is still there in heaven "accusing the brethren day and night," Revelation 12:10. He also came to God in the book of Job when the "sons of God" gathered. In the Gospel of Luke 10:18, Christ said, "I saw Satan as lightening fall from heaven." He was quoting what would be written in the book of Revelation years later and what was to take place at the end of this age. Satan is the "Prince and power of the air," Ephesians 2:2. When he is kicked out of heaven, the angel says in Revelation 12:12, "Woe to the inhabitants of the earth and sea; for the devil has come down to you, having **great wrath**, because he knows he has but a *short time*!"

Now this is my belief how the Abomination of Desolation might take place, and I could be wrong, but it makes sense. We know by what it says in 2 Chronicles 35:3 that the Ark was put in a hiding place and taken out by the priests and carried to the Holy of Holies at certain times.

The Bible also says in 2 Thessalonians 2:4 that, "The **Man of Sin** sits in the temple of God claiming that he is God." He erects a statue in "his image" and then "makes the Abomination of Desolation," which has to be an abomination so bad that there is war in heaven and Satan is thrown out. What could be so bad that it would cause a war in heaven? It will be something that Satan does that crosses the line!

Remember what Antiochus did? He poured the blood of a pig on the altar. The Ark of the Covenant was not there. It "disappeared" just before the first temple was destroyed by the Babylonian Empire. There is a tradition that Jeremiah the prophet hid the Ark. 2 Chronicles 35:3, says the Levites had a place where they hid it and carried it back and forth to the temple. King Josiah told them to put the ark in the temple and leave it there so they would not have to carry it back and forth. This shows that there was a hiding place. It was hidden because of all the unrest and wickedness in Jerusalem. It was not in the temple when the Babylonians carried away the gold vessels. Since that day, no one has known its whereabouts.

Recently, the Ark has been found! I heard about in several years ago and have seen videos of the man that discovered its secret hiding place. It is not meant to be revealed to the world, however, until "certain events" take place. That will be when the Antichrist comes on the scene. Here is a small amount of the information that is on the Internet:

On January 6, 1982, Ron Wyatt was doing an archeological dig under the hill of Golgotha. He had an idea that it was the possible place that the Ark of the Covenant was hidden. While digging, he came to a small chamber right beneath where Christ was crucified. In this chamber, he found the Ark, the Table of Showbread, a Golden Menorah, and a giant sword (possibly Goliath's).

He said there was some "dried dark substance" in cracks on the ceiling and the same substance had dripped onto the Mercy Seat of the Ark. He took a small sample and had it analyzed. It was found to be human blood. It was also discovered that the blood was unlike any human blood ever seen. In a normal male person, the mother contributes 23 X chromosomes and the father contributes 23 chromosomes, 22 of which are X and one chromosome is Y. This gives human males 46 chromosomes. This blood, however, had only 24 chromosomes! It had 23 X chromosomes from an earthly mother (Mary) and only one Y chromosome from a heavenly Father!

In 1 John 5:8-11 the Bible says, "And there are *three* that bear witness in *earth*, the Spirit, and the water, and the blood: and these three agree in one."

If this is true, which I believe it is, then when the Roman soldiers pierced Christ's side, the blood and water ran to the ground, went through the cracks in the rocks, and then fell onto the mercy seat. (Remember there was an earthquake when He died and the curtain separating the holy of holies was torn from top to bottom).

Something else to note is that the high priest would sprinkle this same mercy seat with blood for the children of Israel every year. When the high priest, Caiaphas, tore his clothes the day he spoke with Christ just before the Lord's crucifixion, it signified that he (Caiaphas) stepped down as high priest. Christ then became the High Priest, after the order of Melchizedek, Hebrews 5:6, 10, 20 and Hebrews 7:11 and 21. Only God could have had Jeremiah or someone else put the Ark with the mercy seat under the cross, so that when Christ died, His blood would have been sprinkled on the mercy seat. Then Christ, being High Priest, put His own blood on the mercy seat after He was dead to atone for the sins of all humanity, because He was the **final sacrifice**. This sounds like something only God would or could do. Only time will tell.

There is a prophecy in Daniel about the **end time,** in Daniel 8:23-26. It is about the Grecian Empire being broken into four parts. It says that out of one of these parts (in the latter days) a "king" would come." Antiochus Epiphanes was a "type" of this king, but the Roman Empire "swallowed up" this area and the Antichrist will come from it. For it says in verse 25, "He shall stand up against the Prince of Princes; but he shall be broken without hand."

Even if the Ark of the Covenant has not yet been found, it is possible that when the "Man of sin" comes, he will know where the Ark of the Covenant is. The Bible says in Daniel 8:23, "In the latter time of their kingdom, when the transgressors have come to their full, a "king" of fierce countenance and *understanding of dark sentences* shall stand up." If he were to have this knowledge, it would fool millions into thinking that he was the promised Messiah.

If the Ark of the Covenant was shown to the world, it would cause worldwide wonder and this may be the very thing that causes the third temple to be built. The Antichrist would most likely be instrumental in getting the entire world to help fund it and it would be glorious indeed. This would make him even more popular all over the world because the Scriptures say he will bring peace, but it also says, "By peace he shall destroy many," Daniel 8:25.

If the third temple were to be built for the Ark, this would cause a worldwide sensation and at its "dedication", all the news agencies in the world would cover the event. Then when the "Man of Sin" (Antichrist) pours his own blood (or some other unclean blood) on the mercy seat, contaminating Christ's blood, this would be the **abomination of all abominations!** This would cause the war in heaven and Satan being permanently cast out.

The Lord in Matthew 24 did say, "When you **see** the Abomination of Desolation." He did not say when you hear about it. The only way for people around the world to see it would be by satellite communications. Christ also said in Luke 21:22, "For these be the days of vengeance that all things that are written may be fulfilled." This "abomination of desolation" starts the clock ticking down to the last three and a half years before Christ returns to Jerusalem.

It has been Satan's dream from the beginning to be like God and to be worshiped; remember what he said to Christ in the wilderness and what he says in Isaiah 14:12.

As the Lord said, "**No man knows the day or hour,**" but you can get close. If you know how God has set up His Holy Days and how they have thus far been fulfilled, you can be fairly sure things will happen on or near these days. However, He does say that He will **shorten these days** for His people's sake, Matthew 24:22.

If He died on Passover and was the First Fruits and He sent His Spirit on Pentecost, it is likely that He will sound the trumpet or Shofar (a ram's horn) on the Feast of Trumpets. This is the time Christ sends out His angels and gathers His elect, Matthew 24:31. It is also plausible that He will return to Jerusalem with His saints (Jude 14), very close to the Feast of Tabernacles. There is also one other reason to believe this and I will explain it in the following chapter about the battle at Armageddon. He definitely cannot come after the time He has determined, to fulfill everything. For He says there will be 1,260 days or three and one-half years from the time of the Abomination of Desolation until the time that He returns to set up His Kingdom.

What is the **Great Tribulation** and will "the church" be "**raptured** out" before it begins? I first read the book of Revelation when I was fourteen, and I remember how strange it sounded and how difficult it was to understand. As I grew older, I remember going to churches and hearing many different ideas on when the resurrection would take place and if we would be "taken out" before the Tribulation, during it, or after it was over. It was then that I began to study for myself.

First, what is the Great Tribulation? Christ speaks of it, and it is in the Old Testament as "Jacob's Trouble". The Lord Himself said in Matthew 24:21, "For then shall be **Great Tribulation**, such as was not since the beginning of the world to this time, no, nor ever shall be. And except those days should be shortened, there should no flesh be saved." The "man of sin" the Antichrist, makes a covenant (peace agreement) with Israel for one week (prophetic for seven years) and in the middle of the week (three and one-half years), he makes the abomination of desolation, Daniel 9:27. Most of the world will think that he is the Messiah until he shows his true colors and is revealed. The Bible says, "He shall magnify himself in his heart and by *peace* destroy many," Daniel 8:25. 1 Thessalonians 5:3, "For when they say, 'Peace and safety,' then sudden destruction will come upon them as travail upon a woman with child (childbirth), and they shall not escape." This "travail" is another word for The Great Tribulation. It then begins and lasts for 42 months, Revelation 11:22 and 13:5.

Many people get the **Great Tribulation** and **God's Wrath** mixed up. The Great Tribulation is **"Satan's Wrath"** on God's people, and God's Wrath is on the wicked or Satan's people; two totally different things. The Great Tribulation begins first, and before it is over, God's Wrath begins, so they are going on at the same time for a while.

It will be as it was in Egypt when God poured out the plagues to make Pharaoh let the children of Israel go. Pharaoh was putting burdens on the children of Israel at the same time God was punishing Egypt.

Christ was very clear in Matthew 24, Mark 13 and Luke 21, about what was going to happen. He said in Matthew 24:29, **"Immediately after the tribulation of those days,** shall the sun be darkened and the moon shall not give her light and the stars shall fall from heaven and the powers of heaven shall be shaken. Verse 30 continues, "And **then** will appear the sign of the **coming of the Son of Man!"**

Then in verse 31, it says, "And He shall **send out His angels** with a great sound of a **trumpet**, and they shall **gather together His elect** (His saints) from the four winds, from one end of heaven to the other." This is the resurrection of the dead and the changing of those "who are alive and remain," 1 Thessalonians 4:15 and 17. It is the **one and only time** that His people are taken or carried to meet Him in the air! This is the true "rapture."

In 2 Thessalonians 2:1-12 Apostle Paul said, **"Let no man deceive you by any means,"** and he also made it clear that the coming of the Lord could not happen until **two things** took place. He said that there would be a **"falling away"** first and **"the Man of Sin"** would be revealed! **Whom the Lord shall consume (destroy) with the brightness of His coming."** The "falling away" means that the "love of many will wax (or grow) cold," Matthew 24:12 and 2 Timothy 3:1. People would not believe and not want to follow the truth. In this environment, Paul says, in 2 Thessalonians 2:8-12, "And then that **Wicked One**, will be **revealed**, whom the Lord shall consume with the spirit of His mouth, and shall destroy with the **brightness of His coming**. Whose coming is **after the working of Satan** with all power and signs and lying wonders, and with all deceivableness of unrighteousness in them that perish; because they received not the truth, that they might be saved. And for this reason, **I will send** them **"strong delusion"** that those that would **believe a lie** would be damned."

The Abomination of Desolation has to take place and the "Man of Sin" be revealed. This happens when "so that he as God sits in the temple, showing himself that he is God," 2 Thessalonians 2:4.

Therefore, is there going to be a "secret rapture?" **NO! Absolutely not!** Christ Himself said, "Every eye shall see Him," Revelation 1:7.

People think that because He said, "I come as a thief," Revelation 16:15 and in 1 Thessalonians 5:2, "For you yourselves know perfectly that the day of the Lord will come as a thief in the night," that He will come secretly. A thief is not invisible, he just comes when you are not expecting Him and when you are not prepared. In the next verse of 1 Thessalonians 5:3, it says, "But you, brothers, are not in darkness so that day should overtake you as a thief." Christ even said you would know when His time to come is close, "even at the doors," Matthew 24:33.

One of the parables He gave about His return to earth was the "ten virgins" waiting for the Bridegroom. If you know how the Jews became engaged and married, it is a picture of Christ's coming.

The virgins had to be ready at all times because they did not know what "day or hour" the Bridegroom would come.

The "**father**" of the bridegroom built a room onto his house for the "**son**" and his "**bride**". When, and only when, the father told the son that the room was ready, did he tell the son, "It's time to go and get your bride," did the son leave to get her.

Now just before the bridegroom came, he sent out a "messenger before him" saying, **"The bridegroom is coming!"** The "**bride**" had to be ready to "go with him" in a few seconds or minutes at the most. Do you remember that five of the virgins were not ready and they went to buy oil for their lamps and he came while they were gone?

Christ is the Bridegroom and the Bride is His church, His people. He will have *one Bride* and it will be made of both Jew and Gentile. He will not be coming for two Brides.

When Christ returns, He will have a "messenger" coming before Him. The first time it was John the Baptist. The second time it will be the Two Witnesses, one of which will be Elijah. I have more to say about the two witnesses in another chapter.

Now back to the tribulation period. If you read the twelfth chapter of Revelation you will see that "the woman" flees into the wilderness for three and a half years, where she will be protected and nourished. She does not go to heaven. God will protect some of His people, but they will not be taken into heaven. For He said, "Pray that you may be worthy to escape these things," Luke 21:36. And if you read what happens in Revelation 12, you will see as soon as the "woman", His Bride or church, flees into the wilderness, **Satan** turns and **persecutes and kills her seed,** which are those **"that keep the commandments."** *Most today do not even keep the commandments,* let alone are worthy to escape these things. Are we better than God's prophets, His Apostles, or the first Christians? They died for Him and He said if you are not willing to give all for me, you are not worthy to be My disciple. That is why in Revelation chapter 5, that white robes (symbolic) were given to those that have been killed for Christ until their "fellow servants are killed too." This takes place during the Great Tribulation. Listen carefully to what Christ says in one of His Gospels, He says "you will be taken before rulers for His name's sake, but not a hair on you head will perish," Luke 21:12-19. Then He says some of you will be killed! He just said that not a hair will perish and now He said you might die. This sounds like a contradiction. He means that if you die, you will not lose anything, because when you are resurrected from the dead you will be whole and even better than before. You will not lose so much as a hair.

Another thing that Christ warned you about is "False Christs" or people that say that He was the Christ and still deceive many. He warned if someone tells you, "Christ has come and is in a "secret location," at a certain building, in some "secret chambers" or in a certain city, Matthew 24:26. **"Believe them not!"** For He said in verse 27, **"As the lightening (or light, which is the sun) comes from the east and shines to the west, so shall the coming of the Son of Man be."** (The sun shines from east to west and you cannot miss it!)

In Acts 1:11, it says He will return, "in like manner as you have seen Him go." He will return to Jerusalem, at the Mount of Olives, the same place He left. When He returns, He will have the saints with Him, because He has just resurrected them or they have been changed and been caught up to meet Him in the air. He then goes and fights the nations that have come against Jerusalem, at Armageddon, Zechariah 14:3.

1 Thessalonians 4:16 says, "For the Lord Himself shall descend from heaven with a shout, with the voice of the archangel and with the trump (seventh trumpet in Revelation) of God and the dead in Christ shall rise first. Then we, who are alive and remain, shall be caught up together in the clouds to *meet the Lord in the air*; and so shall we ever be with the Lord." There is an old song that I've heard many times called "Meeting in the Air" and one line is, "For God's own Son, will be the leading one, in that meeting in the air."

We are "caught up" by angels as He said before and are taken to Him. When He said this to his disciples (Matthew 24:28 and Luke 17:37) they ask," Where will they be taken?" He replied, "Where the eagles gather." Where do eagles gather? In the sky or air. This is verified by 1 Thessalonians 4:16 that I just quoted above.

After we are gathered to Him, where do we go? The Bible tells us. He "comes with tens of thousands of His saints" (to Jerusalem, Jude 14), and this is a quote of Enoch! We must understand that all prophecy has its focal point from Jerusalem. We are not taken to "heaven" where God is. This is plain because we "**Live and reign with Christ a thousand years,**" on the earth, at Jerusalem, Revelation 20:4.

Now how will we be "caught up" to meet the Lord in the air? First, He sends out His angels, but many do not realize that He is also coming with millions of "chariots." In Psalm, 68:17 it says, "The chariots of God are twenty thousand, thousand, (20,000,000) of angels; and the Lord is among them." In Habakkuk 3:8, "You rode upon your 'horses' your *chariots* of *salvation,"* (Yeshua)! This passage is a prophecy of Christ's return to earth. It also clearly shows that what the Bible calls a "horse" that Christ rides on or in is also called a "chariot".

In 2 Kings 2:11, "God's chariot" came and took Elijah up into it. Ezekiel also saw some kind of flying "wheel". Therefore, I believe this is how God will gather His children when they are resurrected. If we have to be "in the air" for several weeks or more, we can't just float around. There would have to be a place we could stay. Many believe that we are taken to heaven, but the Bible does not say this. We then must be gathered into God's "chariots." In Revelation 19:14, it says, "And the armies, which were in heaven followed Him upon white 'horses', clothed in fine linen, white and clean. It says right above this verse in Revelation 19:8, that the saints will be "clothed in fine linen, clean and white." This shows that the armies will be made up of Christ and those that are resurrected. The "armies of heaven" are angels, which have just come from heaven to help Christ gather His people. Then after Christ, His angels and the resurrected saints are gathered in the air, they go to

Jerusalem to fight at Armageddon. Malachi 4:3 says that, "the wicked will be ashes under the soles of your feet."

During this time that the saints are with the Lord "in the air", Christ will have to be preparing His armies to go to Jerusalem to fight the earth's armies that are gathering against it. Zephaniah 3:8, God says, "For My determination is to gather the nations, that I may assemble the kingdoms, that I may pour upon them My indignation, even all My fierce anger: for all the earth shall be devoured with the fire of My jealousy."

This will also have to be the time the Lord has an orientation and instructs the resurrected saints and prepares them for the job they are about to undertake. "God is not the author of confusion, but of order", as I quoted earlier. He will have a plan and the angels and His people will be the armies that will follow Him back to Jerusalem! This is why the armies of the earth will gather, it is to fight the Lord when He returns to Jerusalem. In Psalms 2:1-4 it says, "The "kings of the earth will sit and take counsel against the Lord and the "anointed one" (Christ). It says in verse four, "He that sits in the heavens shall laugh; He will have them in derision."

Zechariah 14:3, "The Lord shall go forth and fight against those nations as when He fought in the day of battle." This is speaking about the end of time when the nations of the earth have come against Jerusalem at Armageddon, Ezekiel 38:16-23, Joel 3:14 and Revelation 16:13 and16.

After we are gathered with Him in the air, the armies of earth have to gather themselves together and to come to the Valley of Armageddon. This place is also called the "Valley of Jehoshaphat," Joel 3:2 and the "Valley of Decision," Joel 3:14. This will take several days if not several weeks to move all the armies of the world into position north of Israel. During this time, God is pouring out the "seven last plagues", Revelation 15:1-21. It is in verse 16 where the armies gather at Armageddon.

The Bible even says how God will destroy these armies. Zechariah 14:12 says, "And this shall be the plague wherewith the Lord shall smite all the people that have fought against Jerusalem. Their flesh shall consume away while they stand on their feet, and their eyes shall consume away in their sockets, and their tongue shall consume away in their mouth." This is a perfect description of what happens in a nuclear blast. My idea on this is that the armies that are gathered at Armageddon will try to launch a nuclear missile into the sky to "shoot down" Christ's "chariots". He then will cause the bomb to explode in the sky above their heads. They will then "reap what they sowed."

As I said earlier, God's Holy Days are a "blueprint" or "rehearsals" for His plan of redemption, salvation, His coming to earth again, resurrecting the dead and setting up His Kingdom. The Feast of Trumpets is the day, which represents the "Last Trumpet" that wakes the dead for the resurrection. The next Holy Day, which soon follows, is the Day of Atonement, which means "at one with God." 1 Thessalonians 4:13, "Then we who are alive and remain shall be caught up together with them in the clouds to meet the Lord in the air, and so shall be ever be with the Lord."

At this point, I would also like to interject something about what happened at Christ's birth. It is in Matthew chapter 2. In verse 2, it says that the wise men saw the "star" in the east and knew something great had happened. In verse 7, King Herod asked the wise men "when the star first appeared." Herod then sent the men to find the child and told them when they found him to come and tell him so he, too, could worship the "new king". When the wise men left the king, they saw the star and "followed it" because "the star went before them until it stood over the house where the young child was." This was several months, if not nearly two years after Christ was born. By this time, his earthly father and mother had left Bethlehem and were living in a house. Did you notice that the "star" went before them and "stood over" where the young Christ was? Stars do not move back and forth through the sky, but some kind of spacecraft could! I can go out at night and see the International Space Station orbiting the earth. It "appears" to be just another "star" but is brighter. This "star" the Bible speaks of could not have been a star, but only appeared to be one. It also could not have been a comet because the "star" was there for two years. Furthermore, comets move in a straight line and do not move back and forth. It had to be one of God's "chariots"!

This is what the Bible says will happen when the Lord returns and gathers His saints unto Him: The sun goes out, turns black and does not shine. The moon turns blood red and then also goes out. Then there is an earthquake, that moves the tectonic plates of the earth, and the quake is so terrible that the earth wobbles like a drunkard so the stars appear to be falling. The sky is rolled back with a "great noise" like a scroll to reveal Christ's coming, and "Every eye shall see Him." The rich men, mighty men and all the wicked will run and hide in caves, in mountains; and cry for the rocks and mountains to fall on them to hide them from His face. Then, the Lord descends from heaven with a shout and the cry of the archangel and the trump of God. Suddenly the sky is filled with millions and millions of His fiery chariots as angels are sent out to gather His people. In addition, countless millions are changed in "a twinkling of an eye" and millions more are resurrected from the grave! I do not think you can call that a "secret coming!"

Therefore, if **anyone** tells you that there is going to be a "secret rapture", they do not know the Scriptures or the power of God!

I said this earlier but it bears repeating. Many Christians, if not most, will go through the Great

Tribulation. If you read in Revelation 3:18 it says, "I counsel thee to buy me gold that has been tried in the fire."

He is speaking to some of "the church", His true people at the time just before He returns. He is saying to them that because they think they are all right and are rich, He will try them in the fire of the Great Tribulation to purify them.

Do you know what will happen to the millions of people who have been "deceived" when the Antichrist comes with all his lying wonders at the end time? The Bible says in Matthew 24:24, that he will be so persuasive that "if it were possible even the very elect would be deceived!"

When these **"preachers"** have deceived people and the tribulation comes upon the earth to "try everyone living," Revelation 3:10, the people will turn against them and maybe even God. Therefore, it is much better to "pray that you will be worthy to escape these things." It is true that the Lord does also promise in verse 10 that, *"Because you have kept the Words of My patience, I will also keep you from the hour of temptation, which shall come upon all the world, to try them that dwell upon the earth!"* Keep praying and keep His commandments!

No, there is not going to be a secret rapture. The Scriptures are very clear about this. Study it for yourselves.

Are there any Scriptures that say how the Lord *will* appear when He returns? Yes, there are many. As I already said, in Psalms 68:17 it says "The chariots of God are 20,000 thousand and thousands of angels, and the Lord is among them." In Ezekiel 1:15-16 and 10:9-22 it speaks of a "wheel within a wheel and lightening and wings that don't move as it flies forward. These sound like some kind of spaceship. Again, as I quoted earlier, in 2 Kings 2:11 it talks about "a chariot of fire". In Psalms 18, it speaks of the darkness of the sky (outer space) being His secret place from where He comes from. It also says that before Him will be thick clouds and fire shooting forth. As I quoted earlier Revelation 19:14 says, "The armies of heaven followed Him upon "white horses"'" (flying spacecraft that are silver?). Later in verse 19, it speaks about the armies of the world that came to fight the Lord as He is returning.

When He returns in some kind of spacecraft, the Bible says the armies of the world will think they can destroy Him and be gathered at Armageddon. They also want to destroy Jerusalem, God's holy city. This is predicted in many passages in the Bible. One is Ezekiel 38:18, "And it shall come to pass at the same time when Gog will come against the land of Israel, says the Lord God, that My fury shall come up in My face."

When the Lord ascended after the resurrection, He was "caught up" into the clouds. Where or what He was taken into was obscured by thick clouds. The people there that day were trying to see where He went, Acts 1:11. In Matthew 24:30, Matthew 26:64 and Mark 14:62 it says that Christ will come in the clouds. In Revelation 1:7, it says that He will be coming in the clouds and every eye shall see Him. If the sun has just been darkened and suddenly the atmosphere around the entire earth is filled with tens of thousands of spacecraft with lights surrounding them, every person on earth will see Him coming!

When He comes, the Bible says that He will send out His angels to gather His people. The angels will then clothe and escort the resurrected ones and those that have been instantly changed into immortal beings with them to meet the Lord.

Angels may be able to fly, but is it possible that the "wings" that people have described on them are some kind of wing with a propulsion device? In outer space, wings are not needed. In the atmosphere above the earth, however, wings are needed to guide one through the air.

Psalm 18 is not only a Psalm of David but it speaks of the Lord coming and saving each of us and delivering us from "hell", which translated correctly, is the grave. It also speaks of fighting the ungodly and having supernatural powers! In Revelation 19:14 it says, "The armies of heaven followed Him on 'white horses.'" They follow Him in order to fight the armies of earth that have gathered at Jerusalem. Those in the first resurrection along with the angels will have spiritual bodies and cannot die. When they "fall upon the sword they will not be wounded," Joel 2:8.

Here is a very interesting thing that happened to Christ after the Last Supper (or Passover Meal). He tells his disciples to sell their clothes, if they have to, and buy a sword! It is in Luke 22:36. They had two swords with them and He said that it was enough, Luke 22:38.

A little later, when the mob came to arrest Christ, Peter sees what is happening, takes out his sword and cuts off the ear of one of the servants of the high priest. Christ heals the man's ear and tells Peter to put his sword back into its sheath. He also adds this, "For all those that take the sword shall perish with the sword."

Why would this be recorded in the Gospels? Why would Christ tell his men to buy a sword and then tell them not to use it? He knew what was going to happen; he just said that he came for the purpose of dying. If this were to happen today, instead of a sword, they would be carrying a gun.

He had them get a sword and bring it with them to the Mount of Olives for a reason. Just as when He rode a donkey into Jerusalem, it was a reenactment of things that were to take place in the future; on the day, he returns. Because when He returns, He will "ride" into Jerusalem as King of King and Lord of Lords. When he returns to Jerusalem "at the Mount of Olives" first, Zachariah 14:4 and Acts 1:11, he will bring a "sword" to destroy the armies of the world that have gathered at Armageddon.

He said no man knows the day or hour that He is retuning, but He also said that you will know when it is very close, "even at the doors", Matthew 24:33.

Note: In August of 2016, I finished an e-book titled *The Coming Invasion*. In it, I cover what is going to happen when the Lord returns, resurrects his followers and fights the armies at Armageddon. It will be an event the world has never seen and one they will never see again.

Chapter 15

Who and Where are the Two Witnesses?

When Christ returns, He will have a "messenger" coming before Him. The first time it was John the Baptist. The second time it will be the Two Witnesses. It will be Elijah; or one with Elijah's spirit as was John the Baptist; and another, which I believe will be Enoch. These two witnesses will appear in Jerusalem right after the Abomination of Desolation and warn people for 42 months, Revelation 11:3. The world, as a whole, will hate them and at the end of their mission, they will be killed. This happens at the end of the "second woe" in Revelation 11:3-14. Their bodies will lie in the street for three and a half days. The Scripture also says that the people of the world shall *see their dead bodies,* and will not suffer them to be buried. Then these people will have a *worldwide "holiday"* and give gifts to one another. It was impossible for this Scripture to be fulfilled until we had satellite communications. I have much more to say about these two witnesses in a later chapter.

If the two witnesses are to begin their mission as soon as the abomination of desolation takes place, where are they now and could we recognize them?

The two witnesses begin their mission in Jerusalem and end it there. During their three and a half years, they will travel all over the world warning people of God's coming wrath and for them to repent. This is why the entire world will hate them.

If they begin their mission from Jerusalem, then this means they are most likely there now!

Could we recognize them?

No. The reason being is that God "translated them."

Genesis 5:24, says that Enoch walked with God and "was not" for God took him." Where did God take him and what does it mean he "was not"? A scripture in the New Testament tell us. Hebrews 11:5, "By faith Enoch *was translated* that he should *not see death*; and *was not found*, because God had translated him: for before his translation he had this testimony, that he pleased God."

Many believe that God took him to heaven. This cannot be true because Christ said so. In John 3:13, the Lord said, *"No man has ascended up to heaven*, except he that came down from heaven, even the Son of man, which is in heaven."

Okay, if he didn't go to heaven, where did he go?

He is still here on earth! As I said, he is most likely in or near Jerusalem because that is where he begins his 42-month mission.

The Bible says, God "translated him." Translate means to change from one form to another.

What could he have been "changed into?"

The Bible tells us, although most will not believe it.

The Bible says God "changed" Enoch so he would not see death. This means *he is alive to this day!* How can he be alive after all this time, and what about the Noah's flood, wouldn't he have died then?

No, and I can explain why.

The Lord gave the Prophet Zechariah a vision and showed him many things. In chapter 4, an angel shows him two "olive trees" standing on either side of a golden candlestick, which had seven lamps (a menorah).

The angel of the Lord asks him, "Do you know what these *two olive trees* are?"

He answers and tells him no, he does not know.

The angel says, "These are *the two anointed ones* that stand by the Lord of the whole earth."

This sounds symbolic and is. Remember in the Garden of Eden the *Tree of Life* was the Word of God, which later became *Christ* and the *Tree of Good and evil* was *Satan*. Now these *two olive trees also represent two men.*

In the above verse, they are called God's "anointed ones." In Revelation, they are called his "two witnesses," but they are the same.

Enoch also was a prophet and prophesied about the second coming of Christ, Jude 14. When the second coming of Christ is very near, he will prophecy again.

We know Enoch survived the flood and his death has never been acknowledged in the Bible.

Now here is the mystery of how Enoch survived the flood and is still alive today. I can tell you because of what several other scriptures say.

The flood lasted for about 11 months before it was dry enough to leave the ark. During the ninth month, that Noah was in the ark, he sent out a raven to see if it could find dry land. It did not. Later he sent a dove, but it too could find no place to rest and returned to the ark. Seven days later, Noah sent the dove out once again. This time it returned with a branch in its mouth. What kind of branch was it? An olive branch!

If God would have changed Enoch into an olive tree, he could have survived the flood. The "dove", which represents the Holy Spirit, went to the "olive tree".

I lived along the Ohio River most of my life. Floodwaters would often come up during the winter and spring months. Often it would be up for weeks at a time. When it receded, the trees would be fine.

Therefore, not only are the "two olive trees" symbolic *they are real!* Olive trees can live for thousands of years and some are still standing in the Garden of Gethsemane! They were "standing there" when Christ prayed, and when he was arrested the night before his crucifixion!

Many may think this is impossible, but I will let the Bible speak to that question.

Remember what happened when Satan was trying to tempt Christ during his 40-day fast. He told Christ, "Command these stones to be bread," Matthew 4:3.

Satan knew the Lord had the power to change them to bread.

In addition, when John the Baptist was speaking to some Pharisees and Sadducees, they were saying with pride that they were the children of Abraham. John called them a "generation of vipers and said, "God is able to make these stones into children of Abraham," Luke 3:8.

Here is an astounding marvel that shows the power of God. *Christ changed himself into a rock* before he came in the flesh. He was there in the wilderness when the children of Israel wondered for 40 years. This is in1 Corinthians 10:4 "And (the Israelites) did all drink the same spiritual drink: for they drank of that *spiritual Rock that followed them: and that Rock was Christ."*

If Enoch was changed into an olive tree, does this mean the Elijah was also?

It would certainly be in my opinion. The Bible has already said that there are "two olive trees."

Many believe Elijah was also taken up to "heaven". He was taken aboard a "fiery chariot." The chariot however could not have taken him to heaven because Christ said centuries later, "No man has gone to heaven," as I quoted earlier.

The event of Elijah being taken up into the "chariot" is in 2 Kings 2:11-12. As they (Elijah and Elisha) were walking along and talking together, suddenly a chariot of fire and horses of fire appeared and separated the two of them, and Elijah went up to heaven (the sky) in a whirlwind. Elisha saw this and cried out, "My father! My father! The chariots and horsemen of Israel!" And Elisha saw him no more. Then he took hold of his own clothes and tore them apart."

The Bible does not say what happened to Elijah after he was taken into the sky by a "fiery chariot". If then, they did not go to heaven; **both Elijah and Enoch must be on earth, still alive**, but "translated' and **waiting for their mission to begin.** When the time is right, God will change them back into mortal human beings. They must be mortal because they are killed in the streets of Jerusalem at the end of their three-and-a-half-year mission.

The Bible says that a matter needs to be confirmed by "two witnesses." My opinion is that God needs a witness that was there before the flood and another after the flood to tell what took place. Enoch was alive while Adam and Eve were still alive! This is why I believe **the two witnesses must be Enoch and Elijah**. I also believe they are alive and near Jerusalem.

Another scripture could also allude to this. When Christ was speaking to his disciples one day he said, **"There are some standing here that will not see death until they see the Son of Man coming in his kingdom,"** Matthew 16:28 and Luke 9:28.

The two witnesses will not die until Christ has intervened and is pouring out his wrath. The two witnesses die near the end of the "second woe." Could Christ have meant the two witnesses were standing close by and would be there when he returned?

His disciples were taken aback by Christ saying that some standing there would not die and later there was a rumor among them that some of the disciples, namely John, would not die until the Lord retuned in his kingdom. This is recorded in the Gospel of John 21: 23. Christ has just told Peter how Peter was to grow old and by what death he should die, which would glorify God. A few minutes later, Peter sees John following Christ along the shore of the Sea of Tiberias and the Lord was speaking with him. Peter then goes over and speaks privately with the Lord asking how John will die. The Lord knew of the rumor and knew Peter was trying to see if the rumor was right. Therefore, the Lord replied and said, "If I chose to let him (John) live until I return, what business is that of yours."

This rumor began because of what Christ said that day that there were "some standing here that will not see death until they see me coming in my kingdom." Some have suggested that what Christ meant was that some of the disciples would see him on the Mount of Transfiguration and *see him in his glory* in the vision. This however was a vision and they did not see him "coming in his kingdom," as that was at least two thousand years into the future. I believe Christ almost had to be referring to the two witnesses. They were standing there that day and already in Jerusalem!

Another possibility could have been that the Antichrist was also standing there. He has been alive since the Garden of Eden. He is mentioned as being alive and waiting in the wings to step onto the world's stage. He will also make his appearance at the very end. The Bible says in 2 Thessalonians 2:8, "And then shall that Wicked [one] be revealed, whom the Lord shall consume with the spirit of his mouth, and **shall destroy with the brightness of his coming**."

Here the scripture says, that the Antichrist will "see death when Christ comes in his kingdom" This is the very thing that Christ said that day when he was speaking to his disciples about some standing there.

Verse 6 of 2 Thessalonians 2, says that the Antichrist is being held back from being revealed even at that time. When his time comes, he will step out of the shadows and be revealed. By this, it is saying he was alive at that time and I'm sure he was hanging around to see what Christ was doing. I have written an e-book about the Antichrist and it should be published by October 2016.

Yes, the two witnesses and the Antichrist are there and waiting to play their roll in history and it will be leading up to the greatest event the world has ever seen!

Chapter 16

Armageddon: When will it Happen?

I wrote this chapter many years ago and I came across it while writing *Mysteries of the Bible*. Since there are so many Biblical prophecies about the end of time (many that I have not even used yet) I wanted to include this. I will repeat many of the verses of Bible Scripture that I have already used, but in order to tell the complete story I feel it is necessary.

About one third of the Bible is prophecy and much of it pertains to the "end of time" and the Lord's return. Therefore, here is more about what the Bible says will happen.

Armageddon: Almost everyone has heard of it, but few really know much about it. Most agree, if the world continues as it is, it is only a matter of time until all the armies on earth will confront one another.

The Bible tells of it and if you study prophecy, you will know that Armageddon is actually a place in the Middle East. This is where the greatest battle of all time is to take place. But when is this prophetic event to happen? If you take all the prophecies about the battle at Armageddon and a few other predicted events, you will come up with a time. Nature also tells what month this is to occur.

The wise men, by knowing prophecy and natural events on earth and the sky, knew a great event was to take place. Then, when seeing the "sign", of the birth of a "great king," they knew it had happened. There are many more "signs" about the "end of time" and the Lord's return than there were about the birth of Christ.

First, let's go to the prophecies that predict the battle and why it will be fought. Actually, the armies will be gathered together, but will never fight one another. They are assembled to take over Jerusalem; then things change.

Armageddon is mentioned in Revelation 16:16, "And He gathered them together into a place called in the Hebrew tongue Armageddon." The Plain of Megiddo is another name for it, as is the Valley of Jezreel. It is a large, flat plain about fifty miles north of Jerusalem and is the place where the armies of the world will gather.

In Zephaniah 3:8 God says, "For my determination is to gather the nations, that I may assemble the kingdoms, to pour upon them My indignation, even all My fierce anger." In Zachariah 14:2, He says, "For I will gather all nations against Jerusalem to battle." In Zachariah 12:3, "And in that day, I will make *Jerusalem* a burdensome stone for all people; all that burden themselves with it shall be cut in pieces, *all the people of the earth shall be gathered together against it.*"

In Joel 3:14, it says there are, "Multitudes, multitudes in the Valley of Decision; for the Day of the Lord is near in the Valley of Decision."

When we go to the book of Ezekiel, we find out why the armies are gathered there. In Ezekiel 38:12, it says the armies are gathered "to take a spoil", and later "to turn their hand upon the people (Jews) that are gathered out of the nations." In verse 16, "And you will come up against My people Israel, as a cloud to cover the land; it shall be *in the latter days.*"

The book of Ezekiel deals with the promise that Israel will again be a nation after centuries of being scatted all over the world; this was fulfilled in 1948. Ezekiel also tells what will happen to the armies that come against Jerusalem. It will take seven months to bury the dead, and there will be men of continual employment searching for all the bodies or remains. When they are found, a flag or marker will be stuck beside it. In Ezekiel 39:7, it says that God will call "unto every fowl and to every beast of the field." They will be gathered and assembled on every side for the "feast and the sacrifice." "You (God is speaking to the birds and animals) shall eat the flesh of the mighty, and drink the blood of the princes of the earth." Revelation 14:20, states that there will be so many killed that the blood will be as high as "horses' bridles" and a distance of "a thousand six-hundred furlongs. This is a river of blood four feet deep and two-hundred miles long!

In Revelation 9:3-19, John has a vision of the weapons of war at the end of time. This is when the "fifth angels sounds", which brings about the "first woe", Revelation 9:1.

In John's vision, he sees a great multitude of flying objects he calls "locusts". He says they are gathered as "horses" ready for battle (the Native Americans, when first seeing a train, called them "iron horses"). John goes on to say that these "horses" have breastplates of iron (made of medal). Their tails were like a scorpion and their tails had "sings" (poison). This "sting" hurts men for five months. This poisonous "sting" does not kill men, but only causes them to be in terrible pain for a five-month period. (Sounds just like some kind of chemical warfare). It says that the "locusts" had hair (plumes) as a woman. Could this be plumes from a jet engine? The "locusts had "faces as men". Could this be the windshield of a plane, helicopter or even men sitting in the cockpit of a jet plane? In verse 9, it says that the wings of the "locusts" sounds like many horses running to battle. This is what many helicopters, jets or even a multitude of "drones" would sound like.

When the sixth angel sounds his trumpet, the "second woe" is unleashed on the world, Revelation 9:14. In the vision, four angels (fallen angels or demons) that are bound (imprisoned) in the Euphrates River are released. Verse 16:

The reason the four "angels" are released, is to prepare the armies of the East, which will number two-hundred million! Verse 15 says that these armies will kill one third of humanity over a period of one year, one month and one day.

Revelation 9:17, John sees the men of this gigantic army "riding on horses." He then describes what these "horses" look like, "The "horses had breastplates of fiery red, dark blue and yellow as sulfur." Their heads were like "lions" (lions roar) and out of their "mouth" (muzzle) issued "fire, smoke and sulfur." It also says these "horses" had "tails that looked like snakes with heads" and out of their heads issued the same as the other mouth and they killed men. This sounds just like a military tank. The "heads" roar when a shell is "fired" from the muzzle or "mouth" of the big guns. "Fire and sulfur bellows forth and kills people," verse 18. I do not know every ingredient that is in modern smokeless powder, but I do know that black powder contains about one-third sulfur! Therefore, I believe what John was witnessing had to be modern tanks firing. Their "tails" sound like machine guns shooting thousands of rounds, along with tracer rounds. It could also mean that the "snakes" are shooting forth poison, that kill people, too. It says the horses' power is in their mouth and tails." These armies will also be involved at Armageddon.

In Revelation 15:8 the "last seven plagues are about to be poured out. In Revelation 16:12 the Euphrates River is "dried up" (possibly a dam is closed?) This is when the "sixth angel" pours out the "sixth plague", which allows this great army of two-hundred million troops to come across, "so that the way for the kings of the East might be prepared." It says in Revelation 16:14 that this army will then come down to Armageddon.

This same valley has been the site of countless battles during biblical history. Recently in this same valley, archeologists have unearthed an altar where children sacrifices were made to the false god of Baal. Baal was the false god that the pagans around Israel worshipped and the god that Israel often followed. The priests of Baal were the ones that Elijah had the contest with when God sent fire down on Elijah's altar, 1 Kings 18:19-40. This valley was the very place where thousands and thousands of innocent children and babies were slaughtered. In God's wisdom and justice, this is the valley that He has chosen to punish the world for all the innocent blood that has been shed there.

These armies of the earth gather at Armageddon, and then march towards Jerusalem to destroy the inhabitants. Jerusalem is the key to God's plans, so if Jerusalem is destroyed, the world will think His plans will fail. For centuries, man has said that he does not need God and God has allowed us to reap what we have sown. At this point in time, the Bible says that God has sent His two witnesses to warn people on earth to change their ways before it is, too, late. If God allows man to continue any longer, on the path he is going, he will destroy himself and all living things on earth, Matthew 24:22 and Mark 13:20. God, however, will intervene because of His people's sake and save humanity from self-destruction.

Now that we know where Armageddon will take place and why, are there Scriptures that tell us when? There most certainly are. "No man knows the day and hour, (speaking about the Lord's return), Matthew 24:36 says that no man knows the "day or hour", not even the angels in heaven, but the Father only. It does not say, however that you will not know what month or week it is due. In fact, Christ says, "When you see all these things come to pass know that it is near, even at the doors," Matthew 24:33 and Mark 13:29.

As I said in earlier chapters, the key to understanding the Lord's return is in the book of Daniel. The northern ten tribes were already gone from the pages of history when Assyria took them captive many years earlier than when Daniel lived. When the Jews were taken into captivity by the Babylonian empire, around 600 years before Christ's birth,

God gave Daniel several visions. In one vision, an angel of the Lord was sent to show Daniel events that were far into the future. Daniel 10:14, says, "Now I come to make you understand what will befall your people in the *latter days*."

Daniel was then told that there would be "seventy weeks" of punishment upon his people for their sins. The sins that they had committed were the reason they were taken captive in the first place. Many had also been killed before the remnant was taken to Babylon.

Here is the scripture that spells out what was and is to take place concerning Jerusalem, the rebuilding of the temple, Christ's death, the coming of the Antichrist, the abomination of desolation and the return of Christ.

Daniel 9:24-10:1, "Seventy weeks are determined upon thy people and upon your holy city, to finish the transgression, and to make an end of sins, and to make reconciliation for iniquity, and to bring in everlasting righteousness, and to seal up the vision and prophecy, and to anoint the most Holy.

"Know therefore and understand, that from the going forth of the commandment to restore and to build Jerusalem unto the Messiah the Prince (Christ) shall be seven weeks, and threescore and two weeks: the street shall be built again, and the wall, even in troublous times.

"And after threescore and two weeks shall the Messiah be put to death, but not for himself: and the people of *the prince* (the Antichrist) that shall come shall destroy the city and the sanctuary; and the end thereof shall be with a flood, and unto the end of the war desolations are determined.

"And he (Antichrist) shall confirm the covenant with many for one week: and in the midst of the week he shall cause the sacrifice and the oblation to cease, and for the overspreading of abominations he shall make it desolate, even until the consummation, and that determined shall be poured upon the desolate."

In Daniel 9:2, Daniel reads the books of the Prophet Jeremiah and learns that when the word of the Lord had come to Jeremiah that the Jews would be in Babylon for seventy years. He understands that each day of these seventy weeks stands for one year. Therefore, these seventy weeks would be 490 years.

It says in Daniel 9:25, "That from the going forth of the command to rebuild and restore Jerusalem (including the second temple) unto the "Messiah the Prince" (Christ) shall be sixty-nine weeks (483 years). Then it says at the end of verse 25, that "the street shall be built and the wall even in troubled times." The next part of the verse says, after this (the completion of the work at Jerusalem and the temple, which must have taken 49 years), it will be sixty-two weeks (434 years) that the Messiah will be killed, but not for himself. At this point the clock stops.

"From the going forth of the command to rebuild Jerusalem and the temple, until the death of the Messiah, will be 483 years." There will be seven more years left to fulfil this prophecy. King Cyrus of Persia gave the command to rebuild Jerusalem and he let the Jews return there.

The book of Isaiah was written long before Persia was an empire and before the captivity of the Jews in Babylon. However, in chapter 44:28 and 45:1 it says, "Cyrus will rebuild Jerusalem!" This was written hundreds of years before he was born!

When Christ came 483 years after the order went forth to rebuild Jerusalem, he rode into the city on the donkey. Four days later, he was put to death. He was rejected, but when this "prince" (the Antichrist) comes he will be welcomed. Christ Himself said in John 5:43, "I come in My Father's name and you don't receive Me. If *another* shall come in *his* own name, *him* you shall receive."

The following verse Daniel 9:26 says, "And the people of the *prince* (Antichrist) that shall come shall destroy the city and the sanctuary, and the end thereof shall be with a flood, and unto the end of the war *desolations* are determined."

The second part of the verse says, "And he (the prince) shall confirm the 'covenant' with many for *one week*", (seven years). This is a seven-year covenant, treaty or *peace agreement* that this *prince* makes with the Jews and many others. This is when the clock starts to tick down the last "week" or last seven years. Then in the *middle of the week* he shall cause the sacrifice of the oblation to cease and for the overspreading of *abominations* he shall make it desolate even until the consummation, and that determined shall be poured upon the desolate." In simple terms, what the "prince" (the Antichrist) does in the temple of God will be so bad that it will cause destruction and trouble that will come upon the entire world. There will never be a time of trouble or "tribulation" like it, Matthew 24:21. I explained it more in the previous chapter.

The "middle of this week" or seven-year period, leaves three and a half years or forty-two months or one-thousand, two-hundred and sixty days left. This is the time that all will be fulfilled. Matthew 24:15, "Therefore, when you see the abomination of desolation spoken of by Daniel the prophet flee into the mountain for these are the days of vengeance that all should be fulfilled."

This three-and-a-half-year period is the time that starts the Great Tribulation and at the end, God's wrath. I explained earlier that the Tribulation is *Satan's wrath* on God's people and *God's wrath* is on the wicked or Satan's people.

Jerusalem will be "trodden under foot for forty-two months, Revelation 11:2. This is also when the two witnesses appear and start their mission. During this time, they preach and warn people for one thousand, two-hundred and sixty days", Revelation 11:3. The days that Elijah held back the rain, was also three years and six months, James

5:17. The time the "two witnesses" are lying dead in the streets of Jerusalem is three and a half days, Revelation 11:9. The time the "woman" flees into the wilderness is one-thousand, two-hundred and sixty days, or "a time (one year) times (two years) and a half time (six months) Revelation 12:14.

This shows that during the last half of this "week" is when all the prophecies about the end of time will be fulfilled. That is what Christ said in Matthew 24:15. I explained much about the "abomination" earlier in the chapter, "When is Christ Returning?"

I also explained earlier about God's Holy Days and that during the seventh month (Tishri) is the Feast of Trumpets. This Holy day represents the trumpet blast that will "wake the dead' in the resurrection. That this is the seventh month is no coincidence. The book of Revelation is full of sevens: Seven angels; seven Spirits of God, seven trumpets; seven last plagues; seven thunders; seven stars; seven churches and many more.

This seventh month is when God's last three Holy Days take place. During this month is when the Lord will come and resurrect the dead (His people); and those alive in Christ will be changed into immortal beings, gathered up to Himself and go to Jerusalem and fight at Armageddon. After this battle of the ages, He will stay and live with us for a thousand years.

Here is what I have explained so far in a nutshell: The "covenant" that the Antichrist signs with Israel and the world will be on or near Yom Kippur, (late summer or early fall). Three and a half years later, it will be on or near Passover. This is when the "abomination of desolation" will take place. Three and a half years after this, is when the "seventh" month begins and during this time (late summer or early fall), the battle at Armageddon will occur. This then will be seven full years, the "one week" that is left in the 69 weeks that is spoken of in the book of Daniel.

If you read in Ezekiel 39:17 and other Scriptures about the battle at Armageddon, it also tells you that the birds of prey and vultures will come and feast on the dead. In late summer, at the **same time** that the **Feast of Tabernacles** takes place is also during the fall migration of these birds! All the birds of prey in Europe and Asia funnel down over Israel on their way south! This is more proof that the battle at Armageddon will be fought around late summer or early autumn. "And He gathered them together in a place called in the Hebrew tongue, Armageddon."

Chapter 17

The Coming of the Lord

Here is something I wrote back in the early 1970's. I went through the Scriptures and put together several verses about the Lord's return. I recorded this on a cassette tape (which I still have). I had a record playing of Anita Bryant singing "The Battle Hymn of the Republic" in the background, as I did a dramatic reading of these Scriptures. You will notice an * at the end of one line. This is because at this point on the tape a "sound" that I did not record is heard. I do not know what this phenomenon was, or why it came on the tape at this precise moment, but it sounds just like "three shots" fired from a weapon on a spaceship." I made this recording long before the movie "Star Wars" came out.

"And I saw heaven opened and behold a white horse; and He that sat on Him was called Faithful and True, and in righteousness He does judge and make war!"

"His eyes were as a flame of fire, and on His head, He had a name written that no man knew but He Himself. And He was clothed with a vesture dipped in blood: and His name is called, The Word of God!"

"And the armies, which were in heaven, followed Him upon white horses, clothed in fine linen, white and clean. And out of His mouth goes a sharp sword, that with it He should smite the nations; and He shall rule them with a rod of iron; and He treads the winepress of the fierceness and wrath of Almighty God."

"And He has on His vesture and on His thigh a name written, King of Kings and Lord of Lords."

"And I beheld, when He had opened the sixth seal, and lo, there was an earthquake; and the sun became black as sackcloth of hair, and the moon became as blood; and the stars of heaven fell unto the earth, even as a fig tree casts her untimely figs when she is shaken by a mighty wind!"

"And the heaven departed also as a scroll when it is rolled together; and every mountain and island was moved out of their places!"

"And the kings of the earth, and the chief captains, and the great men, and rich men, and the mighty men, and every bondman and every free man hid themselves in the dens and in the rocks of the mountains. Then they said to the mountains and rocks, 'Fall on us and hide us from the face of the man that sits on the throne, and from the wrath of the Lamb. For the great day of His wrath has come, and who shall be able to stand.'

"And it shall come to pass, at the same time when Gog shall come against the land of Israel," says the Lord God, "that my fury shall come up in my face. For in my jealousy and in the fire of my wrath have I spoken. Surely, in that day, there shall be a great shaking in the land of Israel. So that the fishes of the sea, and the fowls of the heaven, and the beasts of the field, and all creeping things that creep upon the earth shall shake at my presence, and the mountains shall be thrown down, and the steep places shall fall, and every wall shall fall to the ground."

"Thus, will I magnify myself, and sanctify myself; and I will be known in the eyes of many nations, and they will know that I am the Lord!"

"Then the earth shook and trembled; the foundations also, and the hills moved and were shaken, because He was wroth."

"He bowed the heavens also, and came down; and darkness was under His feet. And He rode upon a cherub, and did fly; yea He did fly upon the wings of the wind. He made darkness His secret place; His pavilion round about Him was dark waters and thick clouds of the skies. At the brightness that was before Him, His thick clouds passed hailstones and coals of fire. The Lord also thundered in the heavens and the Highest gave His voice: hailstones and coals of fire." * *(three "shots" came on tape)*

"And the Lord shall utter His voice before His army. The appearance of them is as the appearance of horses, and as horsemen so shall they run. A fire devours before them, and behind them, a flame burns. The land is as the Garden of Eden before them, and behind them a desolate wilderness; yea and nothing shall escape them. Before their face, the people shall be much pained; all faces shall gather blackness. Yes, and the Lord shall utter His voice before His army, for His camp is very great; for He is strong that executes His word; for the day of the Lord is great and very terrible, and **who will be able to stand!"**

Chapter 18

The Millennium

What is the millennium? Millennium means a thousand years. This is the time the Lord Himself will rule the earth when He returns and sets up His Kingdom. His prayer when He was here the first time was "Thy Kingdom come, *thy* will be done on earth as it is in heaven."

This is spoken of in Revelation 20, verses 2 through 7. In verse six, it says that those of the first resurrection will reign with Christ as priests for one thousand years.

This time period is mentioned also in Isaiah 9:6, "For unto us a child is born, unto us a son is given and the government shall be upon His shoulder..."

What will the millennium be like? Many Scriptures tell us some of the things that will be going on during this time and the conditions of the world.

First, we should understand that this period will begin right after the Lord's physical return to the earth. In Acts 1:11, two angels were with those that were watching the Lord ascend into the heavens. As the people were looking at the sky, watching the Lord disappear into the clouds, the angels spoke. They told the ones standing there, that the same Lord that had just ascended into the heavens would in like manner return, "As you have seen Him go."

He left from the Mount of Olives, which is east of Jerusalem. In Zachariah 14:4, it says that His feet will once again stand in the same place where He left. This is when the Battle of Armageddon is taking place. I talk about how and when this battle unfolds in other places.

Soon after He arrives, the battle is over and Satan is bound for one thousand years, Revelation 20:2 and 20:7.

Peace can finally come to earth. Many of the wicked are now dead and the first resurrection has just taken place. The Lord will then set up His headquarters and seat of government in Jerusalem. From here, He will rule the world and He will rule with a "rod of iron", Revelation 2:27, 12:5 and 19:15.

He will have to rule with absolute power because the people that have survived and were not worthy to be changed into immortal beings at His return will not follow Him unless they are made to. He will have to force them to do the right things, which will bring them joy and happiness. After a while, the people will see that God is doing these things for their own benefit and peace and contentment will come to the entire earth. This is in Isaiah 11:5-9. God will actually change the behavior of animals and the way they eat and live. The wolf will lie down beside a lamb, a leopard with a young goat, and a lion will be beside a calf. It also says the bear and cow will feed together and their young lie down together. The lion will eat grass and straw like an ox. A nursing child will be able to pick up a deadly snake or a small child play with a scorpion and they will not be harmed. In verse 9, "They shall not hurt nor destroy in all of my holy mountain, for the earth shall be full of the knowledge of the Lord as the waters cover the sea."

Birds and animals will be so tame that we will be able walk up and pet them, play with their young, and even call them to us. The entire world will be at rest, Isaiah 14:7.

There will no longer be hurricanes, tornadoes, earthquakes, droughts or terrible floods that kill people. God will only use natural disasters when He is trying to correct a nation (Zechariah 14:18) and the only one mentioned is a drought.

Humans will once again return to a vegetarian diet as will all creatures on earth Genesis 1:29- 30. This means there will no longer be slaughterhouses and farms where the animals are overcrowded and or abused. Most likely we will still drink milk, eat eggs and honey, which will not be killing an animal but only using what they produce.

There will finally be peace and harmony on the earth. There will be no illnesses, no cancer, heart disease, mental illness or any such afflictions as they are today. People will live to be old. One hundred years will be the life expectancy, Isaiah 65:20, and there will be no more infant deaths.

Children will again play in the streets of Jerusalem without fear, Zechariah 8:4-5. There will be death, however, because death will be the "last enemy" destroyed. It will be destroyed after the thousand years are over Revelation 21:4 and 1 Corinthians 15:26. I speak of this in another chapter.

We need to understand why the world will come to the brink of destroying itself. The book of Daniel gives the answer. Daniel 2:31-45 tells us that the entire world be under the influence of the "Babylonian system". This means the world is ruled by greed and selfishness and will be this way until God brings His Kingdom to earth. From the beginning, man has loved power, prestige and influence, and has done whatever was necessary to get it. This meant lying, cheating, stealing, murder and oppressing the poor or weak; whatever it took to get the desires of the selfish and greedy heart. That is why the Bible says, "The love of money is the root of all evil," 1 Timothy 6:10, not money itself, but the love of it. This is because if one loves money, and what it will give them, they will do everything and anything to obtain it, even if it means hurting others.

When the Lord returns, and sets up His Kingdom, this "old system" of greed and selfishness will be a thing of the past. People will care for one another and look out for one another.

What else will be going on during the millennium? There are many things. It will take people seven months just to bury the dead after the battle at Armageddon, Ezekiel 39:14. It will take seven years to clean up all the destroyed machines of war near Jerusalem and burn all the fuel in the fuel tanks, Ezekiel 39:10.

They will then take the implements of war such as trucks, tanks and planes, and use them to manufacture plows, tractors and other tools to cultivate the land, Isaiah 2:4 and Micah 4:3.

After Armageddon, there will be no more war, Isaiah 2:4. All weapons will be destroyed, from missiles to machine guns to nuclear bombs. Even small arms will no longer be needed for protection or for hunting. Most likely, the only explosives that will ever be used will be for construction projects and demolition jobs.

There will be no more slums in huge cities. After the destruction, caused by the largest earthquake that has struck the planet since man has been on it (Revelation 16:18), the cities and towns will have to be rebuilt. This time, however, the streets will be wide and straight and there will not be bad parts of towns. Cities will not be as large as they are today; therefore, some of the problems that afflict the giant cities now will no longer exist. In addition, the population of the planet will be only a fraction of what is once was. This will be because there will be few people left after all the wars, plagues, famines, diseases and earthquakes during the close of this age. During the thousand years, however, the population will rise so by the end, there will be a great number of people once again on the earth, Revelation 20:8.

There will be no crime and you will not have to worry about locking your door at night or leaving your keys in your vehicle. There will be no need of jails or prisons. If any crime is committed, there will be swift justice. Lawyers will no longer be needed and no one will get off because of a technicality. The Lord Himself will be on earth, as will millions of resurrected people who will be here to help in ruling. There will be no secret crimes of any kind because people will not be able to lie their way out of wrongdoing.

Hospitals, along with doctors and nurses will also be a thing of the past. With millions of celestial beings here, an injury or even premature death could be almost instantly dealt with.

During the millennium, God will reinstate His Holy Days for the whole world to observe. This is in Zechariah 14: 16-19. Here it is speaking of the Feast of Tabernacles, which is God's Holy Day that is now a rehearsal for His coming kingdom and seat of government in Jerusalem. At that time, however, it will be actually happening. The Sabbath, which is the seventh day of the week, will be observed because God Himself set it aside for man's rest. The seven-year Sabbaths will also be observed. This was instituted for the land to have a rest every seven years, Leviticus 25:4. Leviticus 26:34 also speaks about it because the people were not observing it. During the millennium, there will be so much food produced in the years leading up to the seventh, that there will be no need to plant on the seventh year.

Every fiftieth year, there will be a year of jubilee, Leviticus 25:10. This is when all debt will be done away with. This will keep people, as well as nations, from being overwhelmed by debt.

Life will move at a slower pace. People will work and they will be paid a fair wage. There will be no greed and selfishness as there is today. More people will grow their own food and preserving it, Micah 4:3. There will be no landfills, as everything will be recycled just as it is in nature.

There will be no divorces and no children born out of wedlock. Both parents will be there to raise and nurture their children.

The human body will be changed back to the way it was before Adam and Eve sinned. A woman's menstrual cycle will be greatly reduced (Genesis 3:16) to no more than twice a year and most likely only once a year. This will assure that no unwanted pregnancies take place. Children will be spaced out and families will be as large as the parents can support and care for. There will be no child abuse, abortion, neglect or unwanted children.

Because a woman will not be able to become pregnant, except for a few days a year, husbands and wives can enjoy each other sexually without the worry of having a surprise pregnancy. In addition, because of no stress in their lives, their sex life will be the greatest since man has been on earth.

Animals, too, will reproduce, but not as they do today. The balance of nature will be changed. What now are prey animals, such as mice, rabbits and deer, will no longer be killed by predators and will reproduce at a much slower rate so they will not over populate.

There will be education for all children, but there will not be all the pressures in schools as there are today. No drugs will be used; no one will be driving drunk. Children can walk the streets without having fear of a hit and run driver or being kidnaped by a sexually perverted person.

The Bible also says that there will be one "pure language", Zephaniah 3:9. This is so there will be no misunderstanding in communicating with other nations. Most importantly, however, the Bible says it is so the people can "call upon the name of the Lord to serve Him with one accord."

Will there be modern things such as planes, cars, air-conditioning, television and computers? There will have to be. God has allowed humans to invent the things necessary to make life comfortable and much easier for the millennium. There will have to be heavy equipment to clean up all the destroyed cites. Tractors will be used to replant grassland and crops. Phones and computers will be needed for people to communicate with one another. Planes will have to carry people to Jerusalem in order for them to keep the Feast of Tabernacles. Automobiles will be much safer and will not pollute. By the time the Lord returns, many of the things that need to be invented will be here. Hydrogen and electric cars or maybe some other form of non-polluting engine will be the norm. Big petroleum companies will not be able to keep cars that pollute on the road. Everything done will be for the good of the people and planet, not for the wealthy to get even more wealth. Cars may very well drive themselves as the experimental ones are already doing. There will also be no need to speed and rush because things will be at a more casual pace.

What about sports? There will be sports, but the games will be played for fun and not to try to destroy the opponent as they do today.

How will people know everything they need to know? The Lord will be in Jerusalem and the ones in the first resurrection will be kings and priests, which will be helping the Lord to administer His government. Therefore, there will be information given every day on how to deal with problems.

All these things, that have been mentioned so far, will be for those mortal people that have survived to the Lord's return and are flesh and blood. There will be millions of resurrected people, however, that will have a celestial body. 1 Corinthians 15:51 says that those in the first resurrection when the Lord returns will be changed into an immortal being. Revelation 7:9, says there will be millions of God's people that die during the Great Tribulation. They will die because they love God more than they love their own lives and God will raise them to be with Him when He returns.

One person that is mentioned to be resurrected is King David. Ezekiel 34: 23-24, Ezekiel 37:24-25 and Hosea 3:5 are some Scriptures that say that David will once again help to rule in Jerusalem.

What will our bodies be like after they are resurrected? First, there is more than one resurrection. The first is at the Lord's return and then the Bible says the rest of the dead will be raised at the end of the millennium. In the first resurrection, those that are raised will have an immortal body. Many of those that are raised after the millennium will be in a mortal body, a mortal body that can die again. This second death is in Revelation 2:21, 20:6, 20:14 and 21:8. I explain more about this later.

Those that are raised at the start of the millennium will have a new body that will never age nor decay. 1 Corinthians 15: 35-54, explains it. We die with a corruptible body; we are raised with one that is incorruptible. We die with a body that is weak and feeble; we are raised with one that is strong and powerful. We die with a body that is not glamorous; we are raised with a glorious one. We will have bodies just as the angels have, Matthew 22:30 and Mark 12:25.

What does this mean? There will not be marriage, for there will be no male or female. We will know one another, however. When the Lord was about to raise Lazarus from the dead, He asked Martha (John 11:24), "will he live again?" She replied, "I know he will live again, in the resurrection, on the last day."

She knew she would see him again and she would recognize her brother, even if he were changed. The Apostle Paul also said in 1 Thessalonians 4:13-18, not to sorrow for our loved ones. He says this because when the resurrection takes place, those in the graves will be raised first and gathered unto the Lord. Then those that are alive, will also be changed in a blink of an eye and will be gathered unto them. If we would not recognize one another He would have told us, but on the contrary, the Scriptures say we will be reunited with our loved ones.

Our new bodies will have supernatural powers and abilities. This is what the Lord meant when He said in

Matthew 17: 20, "If you have the faith as a grain of mustard seed you can say unto this mountain, 'Move to a distant place,' and nothing shall be impossible to you.'"

In addition, in Matthew 13: 31, he is talking about a parable of a mustard seed. A mustard seed is tiny, but grows into a large plant that birds can roost in. The "seed", however, must first be put in the ground. Then when *it comes up from the ground*, it grows and becomes very big and very strong. If we have faith in Christ when we die, then when we are resurrected that tiny bit of faith we had when we were mortal will become stronger and more powerful when we have immortality. Then someday we will be able to move even a mountain just by speaking to it. Christ only spoke the word and a storm was calmed. We will someday have this same kind of power.

This is further explained by Apostle Paul in 1 Corinthians 15:42-44, "So also is the resurrection of the dead. It is sown in corruption; it is raised in incorruption. It is sown in dishonor; it is raised in glory. It is sown in weakness; *it is raised in power*. It is sown a natural body; it is raised a spiritual body."

This parable in Matthew 13:31-32 also has a deeper meaning. It is speaking about the Kingdom of Heaven as being a "mustard seed." Christ said, "The kingdom of heaven is like to a grain of mustard seed, which a man took, and sowed in his field, which indeed is the least of all seeds: but when it is grown, it is the greatest among herbs and becomes a tree, so that the birds of the air come and lodge in the branches thereof."

Christ was that "seed" because he was part of God's Kingdom. He died and was put in the ground, then rose from the ground when he resurrected himself. Because of his death for the sins of the world, all men can be forgiven for their sins. Because he was resurrected from the dead, he paved the way for us to be resurrected unto eternal life. He was just one man out of billions that have lived, but because of that one man he "planted the seed" for God's kingdom. Over the years, his followers have grown and now have become hundreds of millions. In the final resurrection, there will be so many that no man can number them, Revelation 7:9.

Will we eat after we are resurrected? 1 Corinthians 6:13, says that the stomach will be done away with. We will not need food, although it is possible that we can eat if we want to. The Lord ate fish and honey after He arose. In addition, the manna from heaven was said to be food for the angels, Psalms 74:24-25. Therefore, it is possible that we will have some kind of nourishment, but there certainly will not be any waste from the food. The food would have to be completely absorbed into the celestial body.

Since you can never be injured or die, there will be no fear of any danger. There will be no fear of heights, of drowning or any such things. You would be able to walk through fire (remember the Hebrew children in the fiery furnace). You would be able to walk on the surface of water, even under it. You could rush up the highest mountain and never be out of breath because you will not need air. Cold wouldn't stop you and you will be able to walk through walls, stone, or even mountains. You would never need to sleep or rest. Your vision will be remarkable. Now we only see in light. With the new body, we will be able to see in total darkness and it will look as it is the brightest day. Eagles and hawks will have nothing on our eyes, as we will be able to see the tiniest organisms and see things at great distances. We will also see in ultraviolet light and in ways we cannot even imagine. In 1 Corinthians 2:9, it says, "Eye has not seen or hear heard, neither has entered into the heart of man the things that God has prepared for those that love Him." Therefore, no matter what we can think of, God will have things so much greater that our mind will not be able to understand them.

Note: I have a new book written January 2016 called *Mystery of the Millennium* and it goes into much more detail about what the world will be like during Christ's thousand-year rule on earth.

While I was writing *Mysteries of the Millennium,* something was revealed to me and I wanted to include it in this book also. In *Mysteries of the Bible,* I have many Scriptures that point to the time that Christ will return in chapter 14 and 15. Therefore, when writing the chapter about Satan being released at the end of the millennium it became clear to me *when this event will take place* because they both coincide.

When Satan is turned loose on the world at the end of the millennium, the Bible says he will gather millions of people, maybe billions of people, to come against Christ and those that were in the first resurrection. Christ will be at Jerusalem, as will his saints. This tells us that it will probably be during the Feast of Tabernacles because all of His people are there. At other times, they will be scattered over the earth helping Him rule. Christ is coming to set up His kingdom will be at the end of summer just before the Feast of Tabernacles. The last time this festival will be celebrated will at the very end of the millennium. This will be exactly one-thousand years! God has said in the book of Zachariah 14:16, that everyone will be required to celebrate this festival, so we know all those that are His will be there. This will also be a perfect time for Satan to persuade his follows to go to Jerusalem pretending to go there to worship Christ, but on a mission to overthrow Christ and His followers.

This will be the test for all those alive at the end of the millennium and the reason Satan is allowed to be free. He will to try to succeed in persuading many to rebel against God. You would think that people who have lived in a utopian world would be happy and not want Satan's way of life, but just as Adam and Eve thought there was more than what God gave them disobeyed, and so will those that believe Satan's lies. The Bible does not say how long it will take Satan to gather all the people that will follow him, but I would think only a few weeks or months at most. It will take only a short period for Satan to convince people that *his* way is better than God's way. There will also have to be modern means of transportation in order to get the hundreds of millions of people to Jerusalem to surround it.

Chapter 19

The New Heaven and New Earth

What exactly is this? Will there be a new earth or will this one be redone? The Bible says there will be a brand new one and a new heaven also. This is clear, but how could there be a new heaven? If we were on a different planet, then all the stars would be in different positions than they are now.

After the thousand-year millennium, there is the great "White Throne Judgment", Revelation 20:11-12. Just as the thousand years ends, Satan is "loosed from his prison", Revelation 20:7. Why would God allow him to be unleased on the world again? There will be millions of people born during the thousand years that have never been tested because Satan was "bound". People that have been born through the ages that had mental problems and never knew right from wrong have to be tested to see if they will choose God's way or Satan's. Likewise, the premature babies and little children that have died will have to have a chance to grow up and be given the chance to choose the way of the Lord. God cannot condemn a child because they have never sinned, but He also cannot let a child that would have grown up wicked (such as Hitler) be in His Kingdom. Revelation 20:8 tells us there will so many people who follow Satan that they will look as the sands of the sea for number. Satan persuades this great number to come against Christ. They then go to Jerusalem where the Lord's headquarters is on earth and surround the city. The Bible says in Revelation

20:9 that they surround the city where the saints are and "God sends fire down from heaven and devours them.

The Scriptures also say, right after this, that a great resurrection takes place, Revelation 20:12-13. The sea gives of the dead, and death and the grave give up the dead in them. Daniel 12:1-2, are the first passages that clearly speak of a resurrection of those "asleep in the dust." This passage also hints of more than one resurrection. It says some will be raised to everlasting righteousness and some to everlasting contempt.

Most think that there are just two resurrections. I thought the same thing for many years, but the Bible does not actually say this. Revelation 20:6 says, "Blesses and holy is he who has part in the first resurrection, on such as the *second death* has no power. All the Bible says is that "the rest of the dead did not live until the thousand years are over, Revelation 20:5. Christ raised Lazarus back to life, but he had to die again. When the Lord died on the cross, a few people were brought back to life, Matthew 27:52, but they, too, had to die again. Therefore, God would most certainly have to bring back many to life so they can be tempted by Satan.

As I said, after the thousand-year reign of Christ and after God destroys those that have followed Satan, there is a great resurrection. This is when the great White Throne Judgment takes place. The ones that have died are gathered from all over the earth "the sea gave up the dead" and "many in the dust shall awake" Revelation 20:13 and Daniel 12:2.

The dead that are brought back to life in the final resurrection leave the earth so fast that it appears that the earth is fleeing away, Revelation 20:11. "And I saw a great white throne and He that sat on it, from whose face the earth and heaven fled away, and there was no place found for them." The only way this could happen is if the dead are rapidly whisked away from the earth. The only way I know this could happen is if they are taken from the earth in some kind of spacecraft, because they will be mortal beings who can die the "second death." In weightless outer space, there is no sense of moving. The only way you can tell that you are moving away from something is to see an object that you are moving away from. In this case, it will be the earth, moon and stars. It also says in verse 11, "there was no place found for them." This means they will be taken away from the earth and will stand before God as He sits on His throne. Before the throne is a "sea of glass which looks like crystal," Revelation 4:6. God will then judge everyone and separate them, some on his right and the others on His left, Matthew 25:32-33. Christ also said that there would be "weeping, wailing and gnashing of teeth," on Judgment Day, Matthew 24:51, Matthew 25:30 and Luke 13:28. Those in the first resurrection will have a spiritual body and cannot weep, but those with mortal bodies can.

After the last judgment, God will wipe away all tears and there will be no more pain, death, sorrow, crying or tears for the former things are passed away Revelation 21: 4. This means that all memories of the ones that did not make it will be wiped from our mind. We will also forget anything that would make us sad or sorrowful. Everything in our past will be wiped clean so we will not remember pain or sorrow of any kind. It will be as if we were just born and have no memories of our former life. There will not be marriage on God's new earth for we will be as the angels of heaven Mark 12:25 and Matthew 22:30. At that time, we will know our loved ones that do make it, but not remember those that didn't. Otherwise, we would miss them and grieve over them. They will cease to exist, "this is the second death" Revelation 2:11, 20:6, 20:14 and 21:8, where they will be dead for eternity.

In Revelation 20:14 it says, "Death and 'hell' (the grave) will be destroyed." After this point, humans will no longer have to worry about dying. You will either receive "eternal life", which means you will live forever or you will receive "eternal death", which means you will cease to exist and will be dead forever without a chance of ever living again. If you were in "hell" being tormented forever, this would be 'eternal life" although not a pleasant one. If this were true, no matter how bad you were, you would someday pay for everything you had done. There is no way God would torment someone forever. The Bible makes this clear when it says that you will be "rewarded for your works, whether they be good or whether they be evil," Matthew 16:27 and 2 Corinthians 5:10. These verses show that this cannot be the same punishment for the wicked by suffering forever. Each person will have to pay for what they have done during this life; the life that God has given us. In like manner, each one will be rewarded for the good they have done, if they are followers of Christ.

No one knows how long this judgment "day" is. It could be a short time or it could be many years. "A day to the Lord is as a thousand years", 2 Peter 3:8, therefore, we don't know.

After the judgment day and death is done away with, God then takes His "Bride" the "New Jerusalem" to the new earth. It says in Revelation 22:2 that His "Bride" is coming down out of heaven as a woman adorned for her husband.

This tells you that this "bride" is the New Jerusalem. It is not a literal city, but this is an analogy. Each "floor" of the New Jerusalem is a different "precious stone." Christ was the "corner stone" that was rejected, Psalm 118:22, Ephesians 2:20 and I Peter 2:6. We are given a "white stone" with a *new name* written in it, Revelation 2:17.

The twelve "foundations" of the New Jerusalem will be "made of" different precious stones just as the twelve tribes of Israel had certain colorful stones and were on the breastplate of the high priest, Exodus 39:10-14.

If the New Jerusalem is pictured as descending to the new earth, it would have to be one of two things. Since this

135

"city" is about fifteen hundred miles high, long and wide, it could not be a "city" as we think of one. Either the "bride" would have to be descending dressed in the colors of the stones of the tribes of Israel, or the resurrected people would have to be riding in some kind of spacecraft that are those colors or both. When the children of Israel left Egypt for the "promised land", they marched with their individual tribes and had a banner before them so each tribe could be recognized. Psalm 60:4 says, "You have given a banner to them that fear you, that it may be displayed because of the truth. Psalm 20:5, says that we will "set our banners."

I would say that each person that is in God's Kingdom will be assigned to a tribe because we are "children of Abraham by promise", Genesis 15:5 and Romans 9:8. In this way, we will wear a certain color to signify which tribe we belong to. It will, however, no longer be the tribes of Israel, but now these colors will signify the "foundations of the New Jerusalem." Each color will signify a "foundation" which was built by the apostles of the Lord, Revelation 21:14.

After we arrive at the New Earth, what will it be like? The Bible says there will no longer be a sea, Revelation 21:1. There will never be a night there on the new earth, but there also will not be a sun, because God's glory will be the light. We would also have a spiritual body and eyes that could see in total darkness anyway.

It says in Revelation 22:1 that there will be a "pure river" flowing from the throne of God. This "river" is not water as we think of it, but Gods "Spirit and His words", John 4:10-11 and 7:38.

Revelation 22:2 says that there will be a "Tree of Life" on either side of the river that will bear "*twelve* kinds of fruit" and the leaves are for "healing the nations". Each month (twelve times a year) God will give "instructions" to the people in His Kingdom, so they will grow spiritually and learn His ways.

The Bible also says in Revelation 21:24 that "the kings of the earth shall bring their glory into His city."

This new earth will have no germs or diseases of any kind. Nothing will ever die there. And without any oceans or areas where it cannot be inhabited, there will be plenty of space. Today about two thirds of the earth is covered by oceans. Beside this, there are deserts, snowcapped mountains and Polar Regions where people cannot live. The new earth will not have any coal or oil deposits, neither will there be any thing to pollute or contaminate it.

Since we will be on a new planet, the constellations or the stars will be different, as well. There will be no moon Revelation 21:23.

What will happen to the earth we now live on? It is possible that God could have other living beings inhabit it. In the Gospels He often refers to resurrecting His people as a "harvest." This reaping of the "harvest" is mentioned thirteen times in the New Testament and the last one mentioned is Revelation 14:15. A "farmer" does not clear a field and plant it just to grow and harvest one crop. Is it possible that God has "harvested" humans several times before and will again? The fossil record seems to point to this. Many Native Americans believe that we are the "fourth" created beings to inhabit the earth. I talk about this in the chapter "How Old is the earth?"

Chapter 20

What does it mean to be Born Again?

Many times, in the past, I have heard people ask others "Are you born again?" Most, however, do not know what it really means. In the Gospel of John 3:2, Nicodemus came to the Lord and spoke with him that night long ago and the Lord told him he "must be born again" before he enters the Kingdom of Heaven.

So, what exactly did the Lord mean? In 1 Corinthians 15:50 it is very clear, for it says, **"Flesh and blood cannot inherit the Kingdom of God."** This is talking about the resurrection and it says, "Now I say brethren, that flesh and blood cannot inherit the Kingdom of God; neither does corruption inherit incorruption. Behold, I show you *a mystery*; we shall not all sleep, but we shall all be changed; in a moment, in the twinkling of an eye, at **the last trump** (seventh); for the trumpet shall sound and the dead shall be raised incorruptible, and *we shall be changed*. For this corruptible **must** put on incorruption, and this mortal **must** put on immortality." In verse 44 it says, "It (this body) is sown a natural body; it is raised a **spiritual body**."

This is very clear and this was exactly what the Lord was telling Nicodemus. He compared it to a birth. When a child is conceived, there is a tiny egg cell from the mother and an even smaller sperm cell from the "father". Once this sperm unites with the egg, it becomes "one" and the human baby begins to grow and develop. Then at a "certain time", the child comes forth into the world.

This is a perfect picture of what He meant. When we come to Christ and "receive His Holy Spirit", we are joined with God, for He is inside of us. After this "conception", we grow and develop until the day we die and are put in "mother earth". Then, when we are resurrected, we come out of the earth with a spiritual body and are "born again!"

When we are inside of our mothers, we are in "water". Then, when we are born, we come out of the water into the world. In a spiritual representation of "coming into God's new world (His Kingdom), we are "put under water" in baptism and then brought out, which is a picture of being born into God's family.

When we first receive His Holy Spirit, we are "begotten" and are His children, but we are not truly "born again" until we are taken out of the earth with our new spiritual body. He said you must be born of the "water and the Spirit". Being baptized in water (a picture of His death, burial and resurrection) and receiving His Spirit, then being "born again" by the resurrection with a spiritual body is what He meant. Then you will be able to enter His Kingdom when He comes back and sets it up on earth. "Thy **Kingdom come** thy will be done, **on earth,** as it is in heaven," was and is His prayer.

Chapter 21

Once Saved, Always Saved?

Can you receive God's Spirit and still be lost? Yes! Just like a "miscarriage." Samson was one of God's chosen people and he did not even know when God's Spirit left him until he let Delilah cut his hair and the Philistines took him. He did get it back at the end of his life, but if he had been killed immediately, it could have been a different story.

Remember Judas. Judas was a disciple and was even given power to cast out demons, heal the sick and do all kinds of miracles. But when "Satan entered him", he turned from God and was lost.

The Lord said, "Every man will be rewarded according to his works; whether they be good or whether they be evil." He mentions this in the Gospels and says that some will receive **few** stripes for the wrongdoing during their life and some **more** stripes, Luke 12:48. Revelation 22:12, says, "My reward is with me, to give to every man according as his works shall be."

Christ also speaks of those that fall away because of the "cares of this world," or the ones Satan tempts. The parables of the sower of seeds bear this out, Matthew 13:18-30 and Luke 8:4-15. However, the one Scripture that says it best is, Ezekiel 3:20, "When a righteous man turns from his righteousness and commits iniquity he shall die in his sin and **his righteousness shall not be remembered.**" It also says in Matthew 10:22, Matthew 24:13 and Mark 13:13, "He that shall endure to the end shall be saved."

What about different degrees of punishment/ and or reward? Some argue that either you go to heaven and that is your reward, or to hell and that will be your punishment, but what does the Bible say?

The Bible has several passages about this. Luke 12:47-48 says that the servant that knows the Lord's will and doesn't do it shall be beaten with many stripes. The servant that didn't know His will shall be beaten with few stripes.

Hebrews 11:35, which is talking about some of the prophets, says, "Others were tortured, not excepting deliverance, that they might obtain a better resurrection."

Luke 12:33 and Matthew 10:21 speaks of putting treasure in heaven, so you will have a great reward. Therefore, the more "treasure" (good works) you have the more reward you will have. You cannot earn salvation, for salvation is free. Once you have salvation, however, you then "layup treasure in heaven" by doing good deeds. Just doing good things, however, will not necessarily guarantee that you will have treasure in heaven. 1 Corinthians 8:1, through16:14, speaks about charity (love). In verse 13:3, it says, "Though I give my body to be burned and have not charity, it profits me nothing." You must "love your neighbor as yourself." Therefore, you must do good deeds to others from the love that is in your heart. In Matthew 25:35-45, Christ explains that He will judge us by what we have done to others. He says if you have done it unto one of these, the least of my brothers, then you have done it unto me. If we do good or bad to others, we will be judged accordingly.

What does it take to be saved? First, you must accept Christ as what He said He was, the Son of God. You must believe that He was conceived by the Holy Spirit, came in the flesh and died for the sins of the world. You must believe that He rose from the dead. You must repent of your sins and be truly sorry for them. Then you must be baptized in His name. Some believe you can be sprinkled with water, but in the Lord's day, all the early Christians were submerged in water. Baptism is to be a reenactment of Christ's death, burial and resurrection. Some are immersed in water on their back as if being buried in the grave; others are immersed in a "fetal position" as if being reborn when coming up out of the water. I believe either way is fine.

Now the name is what is important when you are baptized. Some ministers baptized in "the name of the Father, the Son and the Holy Spirit." Father and Son are not names, but titles. Others baptize it in "the name of Jesus." The Bible says in Acts 4:12, "Neither is there salvation in any other: for there is *no other name given among men*, whereby we must be saved!" It was Christ that died on the cross for our sins, there is no other that paid the price to redeem us. In Revelation 5:2-5, it says that there was no man in heaven, in earth or under the earth worthy to open and read the book. The angel then tells John that the Lion of the tribe of Juda, the root of David, has prevailed to open the book and loose the seals.

As I said in another chapter, the Lord knows if you are speaking to Him. I was saved by using the name Jesus because that was what I knew Him as. Now I know the truth and His name was and is Yeshua, which means Salvation. This was the name He was given. Acts 17:30 says that God once winked at ignorance, but now commands all men to repent. Repent means to turn around and change course.

Chapter 22

Is the "Theory" of Evolution True?

Most take this as "Gospel" and it seems logical on the surface, but look deeper.

Darwin was the one they claim who came up with the theory. A theory is a "possible" explanation of why or what happens to cause an event. It is a theory and stays a theory until it is proven. Every "theory" in the scientific world has to be proven before it is accepted as fact, except this one. This is because if this "theory" is not correct, then the only other one is that God is the Creator of life. Since most do not want to "believe" this, *they have faith* that everything just happened on its own. It is more than ironic that many have their minds closed and are afraid to look deep into other possibilities. This is not new. The religious leaders of Christ's time also had their minds closed. The Bible says that people will be "Ever learning but never able to come to the knowledge of the truth," 2 Timothy 3:7. I have read that even Darwin had second thoughts of his own theory and said if everything were constantly changing, everything would be in a state of confusion.

"God is not the author of confusion," 1 Corinthians 14:33. You see this in nature everywhere. Every animal is "adapted" or designed for exactly what it does. Just stop and think about almost any bird or animal and how it lives and looks. Those that believe in evolution would have you believe that all this came by blind chance.

Take a **woodpecker** for example: It has a long, chisel like beak, for drilling into hard wood. At the tip of its very long tongue, it has a hard tip that has barbs on it to spear a grub or insect. Its tongue is so long that it splits in two at the back of its throat and then goes under the skin around the back of its head, all the way to the top of its head. The tail of a woodpecker is very stiff so that it can "prop" itself on the side of a tree. Its skull also has a "cushion" in front, so that its brains are protected when it hammers the wood. Can you imagine the first bird trying to be a woodpecker and banging its head against a tree without this specialized equipment?

This is just one example. Every bird, animal, insect or life form is so complex there is no way it could have "blindly" evolved into the magnificent creatures they are today.

Another remarkable bird (that recently became extinct) was the *huia*. They lived in New Zealand and they were a wattlebird. They resembled a crow, but had small skin flaps (wattles) on their cheeks. What made this species so remarkable was that the male and female had totally different kinds of beaks. The male's beak was short and stout, like a crow, but the female's beak was long, slender and curved downward in an arc! I would like to hear how the same species could have "evolved" a different beak for male and female. This defies all logic.

Now take the **bombardier beetle**. He has two separate chambers in his hind parts. Each chamber contains a different chemical that specialized glands produce. When he is in danger, he "shoots" these two chemicals together and they explode! This propels him away from the danger and this chemical mix is very hot and toxic. He can even aim this spray. How could any creature slowly "evolve" by hit or miss chance and develop a gland that would produce the right chemical, in the correct formula, in the right place, at the right time, without a purpose for doing so in the first place? Then on top of this, it only works if he needs it. It is impossible!

The **flounder** is a fish that looks like any other when it first hatches from an egg. As it grows, however, it changes dramatically. One of its eyes "migrates" to the other side of its head and moves near the other. Then it begins to lie on its side on the bottom of the sea floor. Those that believe in evolution say things evolved slowly over millions of years. Can you imagine the "first flounder" having its eye move somewhere else on its head and trying to lie on its side? For a flounder to be successful, it has to look like it is now and behave like it does. Anything "in-between" would not only be a disadvantage, it would be a disaster. I'm sure that a fish one day thought, "Hey, I think I will move one of my eyes to the other side of my head and then make my side look like my belly, so I can hide from predators on the sea floor!"

Those that "believe" in evolution say that birds came from dinosaurs. Can you imagine the first dinosaur that is going to change into a bird? Suddenly one day one is hatched with feathers on his body? Why would he have them in the first place? What advantage would they be? In order to fly, he would have to have all of the correct feathers, in the right place and all at the same time. Feathers are very complicated. Each feather has a strong hollow shaft and very tiny "hooks" that zip the feather together. A bird also has to constantly preen them to keep them clean and working properly. Feathers cover a bird's body not only for flight but also for warmth. Each type of feather also has to be in the correct place on a bird's body and each feather has to be "programed" in the genetic code to replace itself when molting or if one is pulled out.

A duck has feathers, but they would get soaking wet and the duck would freeze to death in winter if it did not have oil on its feathers. Therefore, it "developed" an oil gland at the base of its tail so it can keep its feathers oiled and thus the water will "roll off its back." Even if the duck had this oil gland, how would it know how to use it, unless its brain was "programed" to do so? He would have to have *everything* that I mentioned and all at the same time or he would not be a duck.

A bird also would need hollow bones, so that it would be lighter. Even if a dinosaur had the "perfect body of a bird", he would not know how to fly. You can have a perfectly good airplane, but you cannot fly it unless you have someone that has been trained to do so. Even with a trained pilot, if something is wrong with the plane, if it is not "designed" correctly, it will crash and burn. I can guarantee that if you put feathers on a lizard, he will still crawl over rocks and under logs, just as he did before you put the feathers on him.

Now it is possible that God could have changed the dinosaurs into birds. When the Lord returns, He will change animals so the bear and lion will eat like an ox. He could have done this in the past. We have no idea. God has also designed life to change slightly in order for it to survive. Man has taken birds and animals and bred hundreds of different breeds but they are still the same species. All races of people came from Adam and Eve. The same creature, if it is isolated, can change into different races but you can never take a dog and over time change it into a cat.

Every creature has to have everything at the same time, in order for it to be able to live as they are designed to live. If it is true that God took some of Satan's dominion from him and took away his "play things" (like dinosaurs), He could have redesigned them into birds. If you read about Satan as being beautiful once upon a time (Ezekiel 28:13-18) and his "wings" covered the throne of God, it is easy to see the contrast between the beauty of a glorious bird and the hideous look of a "terrible lizard." A beautiful bird in its glory and a lowly, ugly serpent in disgrace is a very good analogy.

There is also the possibility that dinosaurs did not die out until recently. Scientists thought that the coelacanth (a fish) died out before the dinosaurs even came on the earth,

146

but in 1938, one was caught off the west coast of Africa. As I said in another chapter, there are also hundreds of rocks (called the Inca stones) that were found in Peru decades ago, with carvings on them of dinosaurs alongside people. Many of the dinosaurs were known to science, but some have not yet been discovered. The skin of certain dinosaurs is sometimes depicted on these rock carvings, which have circles on them. It was only recently that a fossilized skin print was discovered that showed these circles!

The Bible says that before the flood, the "sons of God" (angels) saw beautiful women and left "their own habitation," and married the women and they bore children unto them, Genesis 6:2. The Bible says these children became men of great renown. This could explain some of the ancient knowledge that still baffles people today. It also could explain how some of the ancient cities came to be built. Some rocks weighing nearly one thousand tons, which were cut with many angels, were moved up mighty mountains and then lifted into place so precisely that they are nearly perfect to this day.

There is so much that we do not know or ever will, until the Lord returns. Apostle Paul said, "We see things through a dark glass, but then we will be face to face," 1 Corinthians 13:12.

Many scoff at the Bible, but if people would have read and understood it, they would have known things centuries before they were "discovered." The Bible said that God "hung the earth on nothing," Job 26:7. It also talks about the "circle of the earth," Isaiah 40:22. This shows the earth is round and hanging on nothing; that it is suspended in space.

I am not a scientist, but common sense tells you that if you take nothing and put it nowhere you will end up with nothing nowhere. Even if you have something and put it somewhere, it will not change, unless there are forces to change it. Only a creator God could create a universe.

God designed and created everything from "nothing." We can hardly change something once we have it, let alone starting from scratch. God said you could look at nature and see His creative genius. In Psalm, 19:1, **"The heavens declare the glory of God; and the firmament shows His handiwork."** The Bible also says in Romans 1:20, "For the invisible things of Him from the creation of the world are clearly seen, being understood by the things that are made, even His Eternal Godhead; so that they are without excuse." Yes, on Judgment Day there will be no excuse to believe that God did not create everything we see.

Scientists are just now opening doors and seeing some of God's secrets in His design of the universe. Some of the things they are discovering sounds like spiritual explanations right out of the Bible, of how God created and keeps in order a very complex universe.

I enjoy nature programs on television and it always amazes me how they explain how animals are able to do some of the things they do. In one sentence, they say, "it is a marvelous design." In the next sentence, they say it is an "amazing adaptation" or a "miracle of evolution." A design is something that has "forethought". Something cannot be designed unless there is a reason for it to be designed or created in the first place. Blind chance does not see the result before it begins.

The "theory" of evolution is always stated as fact. The ones that say this also say that human beings are no more than any other animal, that we came to be here by blind chance and that there is no God no Creator. Then people wonder why there is murder, rape, theft and other crimes. Why wouldn't there be if there is no God, no one to hold them accountable. Why not "eat drink and be merry, for tomorrow we will die." This is the same thing they said and did just before God destroyed the world during Noah's time. Christ also said that this same thing would be happening at the end of time just before His return.

Yes, the lie of evolution, the "theory" of evolution is considered fact when it is ridiculous if looked at closely. Even a world-renowned atheist said it is not true.

Here is something I read in a magazine. The magazine was quoting from a book and from a man "long considered to be the world's best-known atheist." This man, Professor Anthony Flew, "shocked the world" because he believed that God existed. Not only that God existed, but also that God had to design life. He said this after studying DNA and "the complexity of the human cell." He said since the "beginning of his philosophical life" that he would follow the truth no matter where it leads him." It happened to lead him to see God's design in nature and therefore to see God himself.

Another *former* atheist, Lee Strobel, wrote a book called *The Case for the Creator*. He says the same thing. Even without the Bible, people are seeing God in His creation when they look at the mind-boggling complexity of life and the "programming" of living cells. Many world-renowned people are discovering and coming to the same conclusion that "no hypothesis has come close to explaining how information got into biological matter by natural means."

Yes, the DNA of all creatures is so complex that it is almost unbelievable. In the magazine I mentioned above, it says, "The six feet of DNA coiled inside every one of our body's one-hundred trillion cells contains a four-letter chemical alphabet that spells out precise instructions for all the proteins from which our bodies are made." To think that "blind chance" designed all the genes; genes that do an almost infinite variety of tasks, is difficult to grasp. Nevertheless, people do not want to see God in His creation and His design. They have "faith" in Satan's lie, the lie of evolution.

If you wish to learn more about how evolution could not possibly be the truth, read my book. *Evolution: The BIG*

Lie! Also, remember this: "In order for there to be life, first there had to be order."

Chapter 23

How old is the Earth?

Many Christians think that the earth is six thousand years old, but look closely at what God says, not what you think He says.

In Genesis 1:1, it says, "In the beginning God made the heaven and the earth." What were the first words? God made the heaven and the earth. Therefore, the heaven and earth were here before the rest of the Scripture continues. "And the earth "was" **void** and **without "form,"** and **darkness** was on the face of the deep." The Hebrew word "was" can also mean, "became."

What does this mean? In Jeremiah 4:23, it says, "I beheld the earth and lo it was **without form** and **void** and the heavens they had **no light!**" Without form means in chaos and void means empty.

Now this passage in Jeremiah is when hundreds of millions (or billions) of people are on the earth and it is during the Lord's wrath, during the Day of the Lord, at the end of time.

The next verse in Genesis says, "And God said, 'Let there be light." Now if the heavens were already made, it means the sun was there along with the moon. If the earth and oceans were made before the sun, this would mean the oceans would be frozen solid.

If the sunlight was not reaching the earth's surface, there must have been a cloud of some kind obscuring the sun and He did say He separated the waters from the waters. This means He had to take the blanket of water (or perhaps a dust cloud along with the water from some catastrophe that struck the earth) away that covered the earth so the sun would shine.

Many times in Scripture, the time of an event in one line of prophecy jumps for many years or centuries. The verse about the Lord's birth says He will be born in Bethlehem and the "government of the world will be on His shoulders." Now He still has not taken over the world as King of Kings and Lord of Lords. In this one sentence, there is a span of over two thousand years between the prophecy of Him being born and His return as King and ruler of the earth.

Look at what the Bible says in Psalm, 102:25-26; "Of old have you laid the foundation of the earth; and the heavens are the work of your hands. They will perish, but you shall endure; yes, all of them will wax old like a garment; as a vesture, shall you change them and they shall be changed." This means the earth and all the stars grow old and God changes them as we would a worn-out shirt. This seems to imply that He is old beyond counting.

In Psalm 90:4, "For a thousand years in your sight are but as yesterday when it is past, and as a watch in the night."

If the heavens and earth are only six thousand years old and this is the beginning of all creation, this would mean that **God Almighty is but six or seven days old**! He would be **an infant**. This is **ridiculous!**

If a thousand years were as one day to God, then even if the Lord lived only one thousand years in His time, it would be three-hundred and sixty-five million years to us. The Bible says that He is Alpha and Omega, the beginning and the end.

There is another Scripture 2 Peter 3:8, which is a quote from Psalm 90:4, but adds something else. It says, "One day is with the Lord as a thousand years, and a thousand years as one day." Did you get that? It not only says that a thousand years to us is as one day to God, it also says that one day to us is as a thousand years to God. This means that God sees everything that happens in the smallest increments of time. He sees every "sparrow fall;" the firing of each and every spark plug in everyone's vehicle; the travel of each and every bullet fired from a gun and in ultra-slow-motion! One of our normal days seems like a thousand years to Him because He sees everything that happens down to the smallest detail. Since God is everywhere, He can see things in every way and all at the same time. We only see in three-dimensions and that's only because our brains take each eye's two-dimensional image and changes those two, two dimensional images into one that is in three-dimensions. We can only see up, down, in, out, east, west, north or south one direction at a time. God can see in every direction all at the same time, plus in every dimension that exists. He can do much more that our brains can even comprehend.

Now back to the discussion about the earth. The earth is just one average planet in our solar system, and our sun is just one average size star in our galaxy, which has countless, millions of suns. This is why the Bible says that the nations of the world are as "dust on a scale" and are "less than nothing!"

Many people try to put God in a small box, so they can understand Him. He is beyond understanding in His glory, His majesty, His wisdom, and His ways.

Someone once read this book and made a few comments in a book review. Although they liked much of the book, they said they thought I was silly for thinking God could have an age. John 1:1 says, *"In the beginning* was the Word and the Word was with God and the Word was God."

This shows God did have a beginning. If so, how could God be from everlasting to everlasting?

Before God created the angels, before he made the heavens and the earth, he existed for who knows how long. This is because before God created anything, there was no such thing as time. God created time. Time can only be measured when there is a gap or space between two points of time. You can only go forward or backward from a moment in time to count time. Time is the same as distance. Distance can only be measured when there are two points to measure between.

Before God existed, there was nothing, not even time, distance or any laws of physics. This is because there was no material universe even for any laws to govern. There was nothing but absolute darkness. The Bible says the first thing God created was "light," Genesis 1:3.

To me it seems simple that *before God there was nothing* so when God came into being, He has "always" been here.

Our minds cannot grasp eternity just as there is no end in the universe. No matter how far you go there cannot be an end to space. This seems impossible to our mind yet we know it has to be true.

I would think as do some scientists that our entire universe is like a globe. If we could get far enough away, the entire universe could be seen as a round dot. If we could travel even farther, the universe would disappear. Then we would be in absolute darkness and around us, there would be nothing as it was before anything was created. Since there would be no physical universe then there would be no light, no laws of physics, not even dark matter—absolutely nothing and nothing cannot be measured. This would explain how there could be no end because there is nothing to measure. This seems to me to show that the entire universe exists only in the mind of God. Outside of God, nothing exists, which we know is true.

I hope this explains it a little better. A close friend used to tell me that when he thought of such things it hurt his head. Our minds cannot understand the complexity of God's creation. Nevertheless, the Bible says this, "The heavens declare the glory of God and the skies shows his handiwork." We will not know everything until we meet him. As I quoted earlier, Apostle Paul said, "We see things through a dark glass, but then we will be face to face," 1 Corinthians 13:12.

Here is another thought about how old the earth might be. I once gave a teaching about how Satan ruled the earth long ago. We know by what the Bible says that Satan has been given this world and he has power here. Now if this world has been his for who knows how long (only God knows) then his "mark" should be here on earth; right?

Look at the fossils of long ago, and what do you find? There was a time when nearly every creature on earth was a serpent! The "age of dinosaurs" had dinosaurs that ran on two feet; that crawled on their belly; that swam in the waters, and that flew in the air. The entire earth was "ruled" by serpents. Isn't it more than strange that in Revelation God calls Satan that "Old Serpent?" In addition, it was a "serpent" in the Garden of Eden. The scarlet colored beast of Revelation 17:3 is a "dragon" which looks just like a dinosaur.

There is a Scripture in Psalm 74:13, which says, "You did divide the sea by your strength; you broke (or crushed) the head (seat of authority) of the "dragons" (or serpents) in the waters."

Moreover, in the Garden of Eden, God said that Satan would have to "crawl on his belly" and the woman's seed (Christ) would bruise his head. Most of the Garden of Eden story is symbolic of what happened and what will happen (The Tree of Life was Christ and the Tree of Good and Evil was Satan). Satan, once called Lucifer, has always wanted to be like God. In Isaiah 14:12, it says, "How are you fallen from heaven, O Lucifer, son of the morning. How are you cut down to the ground, which did weaken the nations. For you have said in your heart, 'I will ascend into heaven; I will exalt my throne above the stars of God. I will sit also upon the mount of the congregation, in the sides of the north. I will ascend above the heights of the clouds. I will be like the

155

Most High.' Yet you shall be brought down to hell, to the sides of the pit. They that see you shall narrowly look upon you and consider you saying, 'Is this the man that made the earth to tremble; that did shake the nations?'"

When Satan sinned in the Garden of Eden, God said his days were numbered. Also, in the book of Revelation, in the 12th chapter, he is finally kicked out of heaven and brought down to the ground, or earth, for the last time.

Since he has been given this earth, and is the "prince and power of the air", I am sure he has done many things that God has not liked over the countless eons. His name Lucifer means, "Dawn Light" or "Bringer of Light" and he was once a mighty archangel. God crowned him with glory, beauty and splendor. However, pride entered his heart and he rebelled and wanted to be God himself. After this, he was called Satan, which means Adversary. This explains why he has tried to destroy God's plan from the beginning.

If God has allowed man to "rule" this planet and ruin it by his greed and selfishness, I'm sure that in the past Satan did likewise. If God gave Satan the world to rule (and we know he has), what would he do with it? "Create", just like "god" and what would he create? He would create serpents. They would also get larger and more terrifying with each generation. If you look at the fossil record of dinosaurs, it starts out with small animals and over time, they get bigger and more terrible until you have these giant serpents that walk on two legs; and have teeth like iron, which kill and tear apart their prey. One of the last dinosaurs recorded was Tyrannosaurus Rex. It is somewhat odd that the name over the Lord's cross was in Latin and the Latin word for "King" is Rex. The name of Tyrannosaurus Rex means "King of the Tyrant lizards" or serpents.

Now if God has given man many chances to change and repent, I'm sure he also has done the same with Satan. God had to love him in the beginning and I'm also sure that if He loved him, He would "chastise" him. The Bible says that

God, "Chastises those that He loves." Man has killed off species to extinction and breeds different animals to look completely different than they did before. Now he is doing experiments with gene splicing. Why wouldn't Satan do even more? He has much more knowledge than we will ever have. He has also been around for countless millennia to learn and practice what he wishes to do.

Most do not realize that he has great power. In the book of Job, he brings a tornado and kills Job's children. He brings all kinds of sickness and diseases also.

If you look at the fossil record, it shows one layer of sediment on top of another, just like layers of a cake. The layer above the other has very different animal fossils in them. It is as if God wiped the slate clean and started over. We have no idea how often the earth has gone through some catastrophic event. The Bible speaks about the tectonic plates shifting rapidly, "Heal the breaches" (of the earth), Psalm 60:2. In addition "every island will be moved out of their places," as I mentioned before. Scientists have "theorized" that a giant meteor came from outer space or "heaven" and destroyed the dinosaurs! That sounds like something God would do; and if you look at how God has dealt with man, it is the same. He gave man a chance, but man became evil and then more evil until God nearly destroyed all of humanity by a great flood. Then He gave him another chance. It is very likely that He did the same with Satan.

Did Noah's flood really happen? Christ said, "As in the days of Noah, so shall also the coming of the Son of Man be," Matthew 24:38. He reaffirmed that Noah lived and that a flood came.

Did the flood cover the entire earth? In prophecy, there is often a twofold fulfillment of an event. The first is much smaller than the latter. Adam (who was made by God) was the **first** man and all men came from him and he was made from **dust;** Christ was a man but became a "quickening

spirit" when he was resurrected and was the first to be resurrected of the **many** brethren that sleep. This is similar to the Scripture that speaks about the **first harvest** in the spring, which is small. Then there is the **great harvest** in the fall, when the Lord returns.

In the prophecy of the kingdom of Babylon, it says that the kingdom "covered the entire earth." At that time, it did not, it only covered a small area of the entire world, but the "Babylonian system" would grow until it did cover the whole world by the time the Lord returns.

In the days of Noah, God destroyed man from the earth because of all the violence and sin. His only reason for the flood was to destroy man. The flood only needed to be large enough to destroy man from off the earth. He had Noah to save himself, his wife, his children and their wives.

God also had him to save many animals. He could have recreated the animals and had Noah and his family aboard a much smaller ark, but He didn't. If He had covered the entire earth with water, how did some of the flightless birds get to far away islands? Large flightless birds, called ratites, such as the ostrich, emu, rea, cassowary, kiwi and the extinct ones such as the dodo, moa and elephant bird would have had to be there already. These birds never have been able to fly because they have a flat breastbone and not a keel-type for flight muscles. Some of the flightless birds, however, that do have keel-type breastbones could have flown to remote islands before they lost their ability to fly. Losing the ability to fly is not evolution, but God designed animals to change just like the different breeds so they can better survive. Of course, He could have taken these birds and animals to the islands Himself, but if He wanted to do that, He would not have had Noah build an ark in the first place.

Many scoff at the story of Noah for several reasons. Some people believe the flood lasted for only forty days. It rained for forty days, but it took over a year for the floodwaters to completely dry up.

Another question is what did Noah feed the predators such as lions and wolves? There are a few possibilities. God could have sent very young predators to Noah. If so, they could have drunk milk. Where did they get milk you might ask? In Genesis 7:2, God tells Noah to take seven each of every clean animal. This means there would be cows, deer, sheep, goats, other wild antelope and even giraffes that could give milk. If they were giving birth during the time they were on the ark, there would be milk and young. These clean animals could also have been pregnant when they first entered the ark, which I believe there were. One reason I believe so is that God had Noah to sacrifice one each of every clean bird and animal after the flood. With seven, there would be three pairs, plus an extra one, but there also could have been young being born that Noah could have sacrificed. Many other animals such as mice, rats, squirrels, rabbits would be reproducing with hundreds of young being born. These offspring could have been food for the predators. I do not think this was the case, however. I believe that during the time on the ark the animals did not breed simply because Noah had his hands full without adding more animals to care for.

There is one final possibility as I see it about what the predators ate on the ark. When Christ returns the predators will not eat meat the "lion will eat straw (hay or grass) like the ox," Isaiah 11:7. I believe this is the best explanation, that God temporarily changed all the predators to be vegetarians during the time on the ark, otherwise Noah would have to be butchering animals constantly to feed them. If this was the case the deer and other clean animals would soon be all dead. In addition, all poisonous snakes, scorpions or other harmful creatures would also be so tame that they would not cause any harm to any other creatures.

This is also as they will be when God's kingdom is established on earth.

God designed the entire universe to work on its own and He did this before the universe even began. His wisdom and the laws He made, keep it going without fail. It also would be perfect except for the evil in the world. Someday that evil will be destroyed and then it will be perfect.

It is possible that the flood was a smaller type of destruction and the latter destruction at the end of this age will be worldwide as was the prophecy of Babylon and the "Abomination of Desolation" and many others.

We know that just before the dawn of "modern man" or right before or after the flood, there was a great worldwide extinction of animals. In America, we had mammoths, giant wild hogs, horses, camels, giant ground sloths, saber-toothed tigers and a host of other animals and birds that have disappeared. What could kill a saber-toothed tiger or a giant cave bear when much smaller predators survived? The large dire wolves died out, but the smaller grey wolf is still here. There were giant vultures with twenty-foot wingspans and several kinds of large bison, antelopes and others. What could have killed all of these animals when weaker, smaller animals lived? Some think it was "primitive man", but they were rare compared to now and why would they choose to kill the very large and dangerous, the fast and powerful, when they could kill the weaker species?

Another thought is if people in the days of Noah were as they are today, (and not "primitive"), they could have killed off many animals. Many species of birds and animals are already extinct and others are on the way to extinction because of man's greed.

If you listen to what the Bible says about man it says, "From one man he made every nation of men, Acts 17:26. It also says, "Eve is the mother of all living." It does not say that she is the mother of all that have ever lived. We have no idea what happened before Adam and Eve came on the scene. God refers to the "harvest "of His saints as a harvest of a crop. A farmer does not clear a field and plant only one crop. Some Native American tribes say that the world has been destroyed and replenished several times and I'm sure this could be true. In Genesis 1:28 "God said unto them, 'Be fruitful and multiply and **replenish** the earth.'" This sounds as if it was full of life at one time then destroyed and had to be replenished.

I recently published a book titled "The Mammoth Slayers" and it is my second most popular book. One reader of the *Mammoth Slayers* asked if I believed the Neanderthals that I wrote about in my book were Nephilim beings. These were half human and half angelic beings mentioned in Geneses when the "sons of God" took human wives and the women had children by them. It said these men became great men, men of renown.

I replied to this reader that the book about the Neanderthals is fiction and is just for entertainment. I did, however, say that Christ gave a parable about the resurrection being a "harvest" and at the end of time the angels would come and "harvest" God's people. The Scripture is in Matthew 13:36-42. Christ tells his disciples the meaning of the parable he has just told a large crowd, "Then Jesus sent the multitude away, and went into the house: and his disciples came unto him, saying, "Declare unto us the parable of the weeds in the field."

He answered and said unto them, "He that sows the good seed is the Son of man; the field is the world; the good seed are the children of the kingdom; but the weeds are the children of the wicked one.

"The enemy that sowed them is the devil; the harvest is the end of the world; and the reapers are the angels. As therefore the weeds are gathered and burned in the fire; so shall it be in the end of this world.

"The Son of man shall send forth his angels, and they shall gather out of his kingdom all things that offend, and

161

them which do wickedness, and shall cast them into a furnace of fire: there shall be wailing and gnashing of teeth."

The Neanderthals and later the Cro-Magnon people believed in an afterlife. They buried their dead with flowers and personal items the deceased used or liked. If they believed in life after death, it is just possible that these people could have been "harvested" in a resurrection before Adam and Eve were created. We know that the Bible says the "earth was void and without form" just before he created Adam. The Bible says the same thing in Jeremiah 4:23 as I quoted at the beginning of this chapter.

It is just possible that there could have been many races of men before Adam and Eve. Why would God create the earth for one "crop"?

Now back to how old is the earth? Genesis 2:4 "These are the **generations** of the heavens and of the earth when they were created in the "day" that the Lord made the earth and heavens.

Scientists say the universe is about thirteen and a half billion years old by the way it is drifting apart, and that could easily be correct. It could also mean that this is the first universe or the millionth. We have no idea what God has done in the past.

If you read what God says about man it says, "Let us create man in our image after our likeness." There also is the possibility there were other humans or human-like creatures that **were not in God's image**. In the past, God has been challenged by Satan to "prove" that God's way is better than his way; remember what happened to Job. I believe it is very possible that God became weary of Satan "messing up" God's creation and said He could make a creature that was made of dust that would choose good over evil and love Him. And now we are caught in the middle of that battle; the battle of the ages.

Chapter 24

Can you Eat Anything?

Has the dietary law of God changed? Most people think that the laws God gave "the Jews" are for them only, but let's look and see. As I have said, God chose Israel to give His commandments to, but His laws were already in existence from the beginning. Do you remember when **Noah** took the animals on the ark? Just about everyone thinks he took two of each animal, but in Genesis 7:2 it says, "Of every **clean beast** you shall take to you by sevens." After the flood, he sacrificed one of each clean animal. The dove he sent out to find land, however, it never returned. It is not known if he killed a dove, which would have left one short of being three pairs. Therefore, I do not believe he sacrificed a dove. When the Lord was baptized, the Holy Spirit came in the form of a dove, so it did return symbolically in spiritual form.

In Leviticus 11, God told His chosen people what was good to eat and what was not. Not only did He tell them what kinds of birds, fish and animals to eat but He also told them not to eat the fat or the blood of the creatures He said was clean. He created all the animals so I am sure He knows which ones are good for us and which ones are not. Likewise, He made our bodies and He knows what is best for them.

Originally, we were meant to be vegetarians, Genesis 1:29-30. In the Garden of Eden, God said that He had given them all the green herbs for "meat," (food).

When Christ came, did He change the laws? He said, "I did not come to change the law but to fulfill it," Matthew 5:17. He never ate any animal that was unclean. His disciples never ate anything unclean. God proved this when He gave Peter a vision in Acts 10:14 of unclean birds and animals on a sheet that was lowered down to him. God then told him to, "slay and eat." Peter said, however, "Not so Lord; for *I have never eaten anything that is common or unclean.*"

Many people use this passage "to show" that God changed the dietary law, but if you read all of it, Peter finds out it had nothing to do with food, but it was to represent the Gentiles. Acts 20:28 proves this, "God has showed me that I should not call any *man* common or unclean."

Whether to eat clean or unclean things was something I wanted to know the truth about many years ago. When I began searching, it did not take very long to find out the truth. I had asked God for the truth, and then when I realized the truth, I had to make a decision. Would I follow what He said was right or would I turn away from Him and do what I wanted?

I, however, not only had to change my diet by eating what God said was good, but I had to change my entire life. I was born in the country and loved to fish, and when I got older, I loved to hunt and take game from the field like the Biblical Esau.

Therefore, when I changed my diet, one of the things I had to give up was catfish. I lived along the Ohio River and the creeks going into it all my life. Here I caught many catfish, which I loved to catch to eat. I also gave up frog legs, which I had bagged and eaten since I was nine-years old. Not only did I have to give up eating many birds and animals, but I also had to give up hunting them. I loved hunting even more than fishing. I gave up hunting and eating rabbits, squirrels and all the other unclean animals.

Loving the outdoors, I was in the woods and fields all the time. Even when I came home without any game, it did not matter, for I just loved to be out in God's creation. This is one reason I became an outdoor writer.

In the past, many people died rather than eating something that God said not to eat. Antiochus Epiphanes (the forerunner of the Antichrist and the man that committed an Abomination in the temple) came to Jerusalem and tried to force the Jews to eat swine's flesh. Many, however, died a horrible and torturous death rather than break God's dietary laws.

Now if we humans decide what is clean or good to eat, where would we draw the line? Is "anything" good to eat? What about bats, dogs, cats, mice, rats, skunks, other humans, diseased animals, raw or decaying meat, blood, poisonous creatures, or even more disgusting things. This is exactly what has happened. Over the centuries, man has eaten about anything and everything, even to the point of eating poisonous things, which killed him or made him sick. Some things do not kill you quickly, but causes you to be in bad health or that takes many years off your life.

Recently I happened to come across something interesting while looking through the 2015 Indiana hunting guide. Here is an excerpt from the hunting guide concerning wild pigs: "They (pigs) are known to carry more than 30 pathogens and parasites that can be transmitted to livestock, people, pets and wildlife. Some of these pathogens can be directly transmitted to humans, causing life-long debilitating illnesses. Anyone coming in contact with wild pig blood and organs should take necessary precautions."

Now I think you can see why God said that we should not eat a pig and why he said we should not even touch one.

In the Bible, you may see the phrase 'what God has sanctified.' This means what God has "set apart" for a specific reason, but you must go to the Scriptures to see what He has sanctified. He has already told you what He has sanctified and set apart for humans to eat and it is in Leviticus, chapter 11.

Holy also means to be "set apart" and in Hebrew, holy is kadosh or kosher, and that is what "set apart" food is; it is kosher. God not only wants our food to be set apart, He wants us to be set apart, for He said, "Be ye holy, as I am holy."

Christians all the time say they want to "follow in the Lord's footsteps," and do as He would do. Well, all He had, as did the first Christians, was the Old Testament to guide them and it gave them all the rules they needed.

I have heard several preachers from many different denominations talk about coming to the same conclusion as I did about eating what God has said for us to eat. Romans 12:1, says that we are to present our bodies as a living sacrifice and be set apart. 1 Corinthians 6:19, says, "Don't you know that your body is the temple of the Holy Spirit." It is up to you of course to decide what you want to put in your body. Will it be what God has said is good for you, or will you follow your own desires and eat whatever you want?

Chapter 25

What really happened in the Garden of Eden?

Since the story about the Garden of Eden was written, people have wondered what really happened there. Did the Garden of Eden even exist?

God said, in the Bible, that there was once a Garden of Eden, so I believe it. We do not know for sure where it was, what it really looked like or even if it was a garden as we know one. It could have been a symbolic garden.

The night before Christ died, He was in a garden. While he was there, an incident happened, which shows that the Garden story was not just a story.

First, let us go back to the Garden and see what happened. Genesis 2:8 says, "And the Lord planted a garden eastward in Eden." This tells us it was a garden in the eastern part of a place called Eden.

Then the Scripture says, "And out of the ground made the Lord God to grow every tree that is pleasant to the sight, and good for food; the **"tree of life"** also was there in the midst of the garden and the **"tree of the knowledge of good and evil."**

If we read and understand the Scriptures, we see that this garden had to have been *planted* before God made man so "the trees" would have already been there. It also says that God made the woman from and for the man, which had to be on the last day before He rested on the Sabbath.

When God put the man in this garden, He told him that he could eat of every tree except from the tree of the knowledge of good and evil. He also said, "In the **day** you eat it you will surely die."

Now we know that the day that Adam ate the "fruit" he did not die, so what did God mean? "A day to the Lord is as a thousand years," the Bible says. Does this mean that it took him six thousand years to create (or recreate) the heavens and the earth? Does it mean that the earth had to be restored to where it was before some catastrophic disaster took place? We don't know for sure. If, however, He is going to "live and reign" on earth for a thousand years, it is very likely that the days He speaks of in Genesis are one thousand years long. He says in Genesis 2:4, "These are the **generations** of the heavens and of the earth when they were created, in the **day** that the Lord God made the earth and the heavens.

We may never understand many of these mysteries until the Lord returns. However, if you read the book of Daniel, it says in chapter 12 that "In the last days men shall run to and fro and knowledge shall be increased." Suddenly in our day, we have knowledge that people of ancient times could not even imagine. With this knowledge, we may be able to get a better glimpse into what "could have happened" in the Garden of Eden.

We know, if we understand the Scriptures and what Christ said when He was here, that He spoke very symbolic about Himself. He said if you *"eat of my flesh"* and in another place, He said, "If you drink of the water I shall give you" and *"Out of my belly shall flow rivers of living water."* He uses this same language when He speaks of the Garden of Eden story.

The **Tree of Life** was **The Word, which became Christ**. The **Tree of the Knowledge of Good and Evil** was **Satan**.

Right after God made the first man and woman, they were very happy because they had never known guilt. The Bible says they were naked and were not ashamed. They did not know what shame felt like. Then God tested them. God gave them one "law", one rule, which was not to "eat" of the tree in the middle of the garden. Up unto that time they had no rules.

In Genesis 3:6 it says, "The woman 'saw the tree' that it was good for 'food' and that it was 'pleasant' to the eyes, and a tree to be desired to make one wise."

If this "tree" was Satan, which it was, because the Bible says he was there. In Ezekiel 28:13 it says, "Thou has been in the Garden of God." In verse 17, "Your heart was lifted up because of your beauty. You have corrupted your wisdom because of your brightness," (glory).

When Satan saw Eve coming near, he watched her face light up when she beheld his beauty. She, however, kept her distance, remembering what God had said.

Satan saw her reluctance to come near him so he said, "Hasn't God said that you can "eat" of every tree of the garden?"

Eve slowly came near and said, "We may eat of every tree that is in the garden, except the fruit of the tree that is in the middle of the garden. For God said, 'You shall not eat of it or touch it, lest you die.'"

Satan then replied, "You will not surely die," (this was the first lie and people still believe that humans have an eternal spirit and they never die). Then Satan added, "God knows that in the day you eat of it your eyes will be opened and you will be as gods, knowing good and evil."

Eve then was speaking with Satan. She saw his beauty and heard his "words." When Christ was here on earth, he spoke of taking in the "Words of God", which will give you eternal life. He also said in John 6:53-57, "Unless you eat of the flesh of the Son of Man and drink His blood you have no life in you." This means you must eat the bread and wine at Passover in order to be part of Him. This is an "**act**" you must do to have eternal life, for Christ said, "I will raise him up the *last day*."

When Eve listened to Satan's "words", they sounded very good and very wise. However, she had not yet sinned. Just hearing him was not the sin, she had to "take in" or "eat" His words and the way to do that is to **"act"** upon them. Once she did what he said, then she was "poisoned."

What did she do? No one knows for certain, but it had to be something to do with her **reproductive system**. How do we know this? Because she covered herself later.

What was it that Satan did to cause Eve to sin? Satan has always wanted to be God. He is the "god of this world" as I quoted earlier. His wisdom and beauty went to his head and he wanted to be God and to be worshiped as God is worshiped. If he wants to be like God, then he would try to "copy" God. What did God do? God "created man in His image after His likeness". Satan may have also wanted to create man in his image after his likeness. Many times, the Lord said, "You are of your father the devil." Satan has always influenced man and they have followed him. Therefore, he is their god and father and they are his children.

Satan could not make man from the dust as God did, so besides having men serve him, he may have tried copy and make "a son" like God did with Christ. If so, then he would have had only two choices. One was to take DNA from Eve and then Adam and make his own son. The second was to have Eve bear a child for him with Adam and perhaps Satan's, own modified DNA.

How did God create His Son, Christ? He put His Holy Spirit inside of Mary (who was a virgin) to create His own begotten Son. If Satan wanted to copy God, he may have done something similar in the Garden to try to mess up God's plans. He has tried to stop God every step of the way. He tried to kill Moses and Christ when they were babies. He tried to tempt Christ in the wilderness. He has tried to stop Christianity from spreading. He has "poisoned" God's

Words with man's "traditions." He has tried to destroy anything he could to make God's plans fail.

When God created Adam and Eve, Satan saw his chance. He had the only two people on earth. He had the beginning of humanity. His "pruning shears" were in his hand as he stood in the Garden of Eden. If he could do something now, he could take God's plan and "nip it in the bud."

Whatever Eve did, she and Satan needed Adam. Adam was minding his own business, sitting along a stream, watching the birds and animals frolicking in the garden.

Eve comes up to Adam and says, "Adam, honey, would you come here a minute? I want to show you something."

Adam, thinking it may be something important, turned around and said, "What is it, sweetheart?"

"It's something I want to show you. I'm not going to tell you what it is." She then leads him to the center of the garden where Satan is waiting.

When they arrive, Satan is sitting under a shade tree smiling. Then Satan tells Adam what he had told Eve.

Whatever it was, Satan needed both of them for his plan. Either Satan needed DNA from both of them or he needed both of them to act upon his words. We know that Satan wanted the body of Moses and the angel argued with him about it, Jude 9. This leads me to believe he took some of Adam and Eve's DNA, at least the gene that gave them immortality. This would have caused them to start to age and thus die. Scientists today, say there is no reason humans cannot live for a thousand years or maybe indefinitely. We keep replacing cells all the time. Recently they have found what they think causes the aging and death of the cells in our body.

If Satan wanted his own son (trying to copy God), he could have taken the "good gene" that would have kept them from growing old and dying and "gave" it to his son. I say this because of the Antichrist. This person is also called, the "man of sin." The Apostle Paul said that he was there when Christ was alive, because he said, "we know what keeps him from being revealed," 2 Thessalonians 2:3-8.

The "original sin" was in the Garden of Eden. It had to do with Adam and Eve's reproductive system. Either they had a child for Satan or Satan made his own from what he "took" from them or more correctly, what they gave him.

Some think Cain was the "man of sin". He had a "mark" on his forehead, which God put there. In Revelation, the Antichrist puts a "mark" on all his followers. In 1 John 3:12, it says, "Not as Cain, who was of that 'wicked one'. I believe this just means Cain was not right in his heart, not physically Satan's son. Whoever the Antichrist is, he is alive now and has been since the Garden of Eden.

When our first parents sinned and broke God's rules (law), they felt guilty and felt it for the first time. This guilt is still in our hearts. We are born with a conscience and if we do something wrong, we feel guilty. It is there to guide us. Romans 2:12 says, "For as many as have sinned without law, shall perish without the law and as many as have sinned with the law shall be judged by the law. It explains it more in Romans 2:14, "For when people that don't have the law do the right thing by nature, that is a law in itself." Verse 15 explains it even further by saying those that do the right thing do it because the "law is written in their heart" and their conscience bears witness to this. This means our conscience tells us what is right and wrong. God's law is written on our hearts.

You can see this by what Adam and Eve did after they disobeyed God. After Adam and Eve listened to Satan and acted on what he said to them, God found them hiding. God then asked, "Who told you that you were naked?" There was only one other in the garden who could have told them this.

God knew what Satan wanted to do. He also knew that Adam and Eve had listened to Satan. He had to have known that Satan would have tried to trick them out of their "eternal life". The two had covered themselves with aprons made of fig leaves. Evidently, there was something physical on their body, which showed what they had done.

It has always made me wonder why God would want men to be circumcised to "set them apart" for His own. Could Satan have had Adam circumcised to be his follower? Could Eve have had a child for Satan, or even given him an embryo to "create" his own son?

All through the Scriptures, the "first born" belonged to God. If Cain was the first-born, he was evil and with the other Scriptures about the mark, he could have been the product of Satan's lies or even Satan's offspring. The prophecy in Genesis 3:13, says, "And I will put enmity between your seed (your followers/ "man of sin") and the woman's seed," (her offspring, Christ/church).

In another place, I talk about what happened with Christ in the Garden of Gethsemane and how things were finally made right when the young man ran up, gave Him a linen cloth and ran away naked. Christ was about to go to the cross to die and undo what Adam, Eve and Satan had done. The "Tree of Life" in "The Garden" had a plan from the beginning and He brought about the way that men could "eat of the Tree of Life" and live forever as God wanted all along.

There is also one other possibility. The Bible says that Adam and Eve "were naked and not ashamed." A child can be naked and not be ashamed until they reach puberty. If the first humans were made to never age, grow old and die, then they may have looked as children do. After the fall, God told Adam that he would have to work by the "sweat of his face." One reason men and women have pubic hair is to disperse moisture, which keeps them cool and dry when they sweat. If they lived in a perfect environment (the Garden of Eden) and never needed to sweat, then they would not need to have pubic hair. If, however, they began to age and go through puberty, then they would have grown

173

hair. Afterwards, not having a razor, they would have known that God would instantly notice what had happened if He saw them. Therefore, they "covered themselves" so He could not see what had happened.

As I was writing this book, it dawned on me there is also a spiritual reason, which points to Christ, as to why God had Abraham and his descendants be circumcised. When Adam sinned, he covered his private parts to "hide his sin". Before he sinned "he was naked and was not ashamed." After he sinned, he was ashamed. A man is born naturally with a foreskin. It is unnatural to be circumcised. Circumcision takes the "covering" off the man's private part. When Christ came, he took away the sin that caused death by paying the penalty for sin. Therefore, by Christ taking away that sin, he spiritually "uncovered" the man and restored him as he was before he sinned. He undid the shame. After Christ died, there was no need to be circumcised as Apostle Paul said.

It is not a sin to be circumcised, as there are benefits to it, but circumcision is not necessary to follow Christ. *Christ has taken away our sin and shame* when he paid the penalty for our first parent's sin by dying on the cross. If we believe in Him and follow Him, we need not be ashamed when we stand before Him on Judgment Day. We will be guiltless as where Adam and Eve before they sinned.

If you read what happened after Adam and Eve sinned, you can see that each generation died a little younger. The first generation did not even get married until they were around seventy-years old and lived eight or nine hundred years. Then each succeeding generation married younger and younger and died younger. This seems to show that in the beginning, children aged very slowly and did not go through puberty until they were at least fifty years old or more.

After the flood, the age of man drops dramatically. Noah was six-hundred years old during the flood and lived to be nine-hundred and fifty, Genesis 9:29.

Abraham lived to be only one-hundred and seven-five years old, Genesis 25:7. Isaac lived to be one-hundred and eighty, Genesis 35:28. Jacob lived to be one-hundred and forty-seven, Genesis 47:28, and Joseph lived to be one-hundred and ten, Genesis 50:26.

At the end of the children of Israel's four-hundred-year captivity in Egypt, Moses lived to be one-hundred and twenty. Moses, however, was special because when he died the Bible says that, "His eyes were not dim, nor his natural forces abated," Deuteronomy 34:7. This means that he was in perfect health and as a man in his prime!

In the New Testament, an elderly widow is mentioned as being extremely old. Luke 2:36-37, tells of a prophetess named Anna. It says that she had been in the temple doing service for eighty-four years. She had been a widow after only seven years of marriage. If she had been married at the age of sixteen, as was the norm then, this means she would have been one-hundred and nine.

This passage tells us that being over a hundred was a rare thing during the time of Christ. All of this seems to suggest what I have pointed out. That is, whatever happened in Garden of Eden seemed to be related to a "modification" of the gene that is responsible for aging.

We will not know for sure what took place in the Garden until the Lord returns, but I wanted to put this in here, so you can think about it.

Chapter 26

Who was Cain's Wife?

Many have argued about this and the Bible does not give her name, where she came from, or if she was related to Cain. The Bible does give other passages, however, that must have the answer.

In Genesis 4:1, it says "Adam "knew" his wife (had sexual intercourse), she conceived and bare Cain." The next verse says that Eve had another son and called him Abel. Upon first glance, it sounds like this was right after she had Cain, but the Bible does not say this. Most assume they were born close together and they were the only two children for many years. Let's see if that is true.

Genesis 4:25 states that Adam and Eve had another son and named him Seth, and Eve said that God has given me another son instead of Abel who Cain killed. This sounds as if there were no other sons until Seth was born, which must be true.

In Genesis 5:3, it tells us that Adam was one-hundred and thirty years old when Seth was born.

Genesis 5:4 says, "Adam was nine-hundred and thirty years old when he died and had "sons and *daughters*." This tells us that there were one-hundred and thirty years between the time Adam and Eve were created until Seth was born. The Bible only mentions these three sons by name. It does not tell us any of the other children's names, but does say there were other sons and daughters. These three sons were the only children the Bible records by name for a reason. It recorded the birth and death of Seth to show the linage of

Seth unto the Messiah. These were the only ones that were important to the story.

Therefore, if there were one-hundred and thirty years between Abel and Seth, and Adam had other sons and daughters, this tells us that there had to be at least one or more daughters born during this time.

Genesis 4:3 says that, "In the *process of time*, that Cain brought an offering from the fruit of the ground to God." By this statement, it proves they were adult men by that time. It does not say how long this "process of time" is, but it had to be many years. How do we know this? We know this by looking at the Scriptures later on. In Genesis 5:5-32 it gives the ages of the men in the linage leading up to Noah. It also tells how old each man was when a son was born that was in this linage. Seth was one-hundred and five when he Enos was born. Enos was ninety-years-old when Cainan was born. Cainan was seventy-years-old when Mahalaleel was born. Mahalaleel was sixty-five when he fathered Jared. Jared was one-hundred and sixty-two when he fathered Enoch. Then Enoch was sixty-five when Methuselah was born, continuing on to Noah. This shows that men did not father children until they were more than sixty-years old and most were older still.

We also do not know how long it was from the time Cain killed his brother, Abel, until God confronted him. I would think within a few weeks at the most, but it could have been longer. If we know that the generations after Adam aged very slowly and they did not have children until they were sixty or seventy years old, then we would have to conclude that Cain was near this age also when he "took" a wife."

This brings us to the Scripture in Genesis 4:16, where God drives Cain "east of Eden". Cain then goes to the land of "Nod". In verse 17, it says, "Cain had sex with his wife and she conceived and had a son they name Enoch.

So here is the question, where did Cain get his wife? The Bible says he left from where he was, which was east of Eden, therefore he had to "take" his wife with him.

His wife then had to be a sister, one of the daughters that Adam and Eve had during that one-hundred and thirty-year period before Seth was born. The Bible does not record any of the daughters' names let alone the length of their life. It does not even tell us how long Eve lived or mention her death.

If the men did not marry and have children until they were sixty or seventy-years-old then I'm sure the women were near that age, but most likely somewhat younger. Therefore, if we take the other passage in Genesis 3:20, which says that Adam named his wife Eve because she is the "mother of all living" and that God made man from "one blood" (Adam) Acts 17:26, we can come up with only one answer. That answer is that Cain married one of his sisters.

Now we come to the question, why would God allow this? What about inbreeding?

If we go to the story of Noah and the flood, we can see how God "prepared" the animals that He sent to Noah. Genesis 7:15 says, "And they (the birds, animals and other creatures), went in unto Noah into the ark. It says in Genesis 7:2 that there were seven of every clean animal and only two each of the unclean animals.

The animals that were sent to Noah, God had specifically chosen. There was no way that Noah could have gathered all the birds, animals and insects that were necessary for him to bring aboard the ark. God chose or prepared each of these animals, so that when they reproduced, they would not have problems caused by inbreeding.

When God created Adam, He took one of Adam's ribs and "cloned" a mate for him. This first woman was "bone of my bone and flesh of my flesh" Genesis 2:23. This is also a picture of Christ and the church as I explain in another chapter. A clone is even closer than a sister. It would be even closer than an identical twin. Adam must have been created with special genes so that future generations would be diverse. All races came from him. Noah's sons became the three major races of people on earth. God had to do this because He knew the first children born would have to marry their brothers or sisters.

Centuries later, even after the flood, they were still marring their half-sisters and half-brothers. Genesis 20:12, shows us that Abraham and his wife Sarah had the same father but different mothers, making them half-brother and half-sister.

When Moses led the children of Israel out into the wilderness, God gave them laws concerning who they could and could not marry. Leviticus, chapter 18, explains what is not lawful. It says that a person is not to have sex with their father, mother, stepfather, stepmother, brother, sister, half-brother, half-sister, aunt, uncle, grandchild, sister-in-law, brother-in-law, stepdaughter and other close kin. It does not mention cousins, so this was lawful.

Why would God allow it earlier and now change things? As I said earlier, the first man and woman were special and must have had modified genes so they could give rise to all races. After many generations, the gene pool would become small if there was constant inbreeding. No one but God knew about genes and the problems associated with having children by a very close relative. This was why He chose a special people to make known His truth. He gave these laws so the people would be healthy.

With all these Bible Scriptures, the question in my mind is answered. Cain married one of his sisters.

Chapter 27

Choosing Between Good and Evil

In this chapter, we will see how "the mystery of iniquity" came about, 2 Thessalonians 2:7, and what Apostle Paul meant in the book of Romans chapter 7, about choosing to do right.

The Bible mentions 'mystery' or 'mysteries' 28 times. Some have been revealed during the time of the Apostles and some are being revealed today. Some will not be understood until the Lord returns and tells us. 1 Corinthians 13:12, "For now we see through a glass, darkly, but then face to face: now in part, but then I shall know even as I am known."

In the Garden of Eden, in Genesis 3:4-5, Satan said to Eve that if she "ate of the tree of good and evil" she would not die. This was the first lie that Satan told. He also told her that God knows that in the day you eat of it, then your eyes will be opened and you shall be as gods, knowing good from evil." This second part was not a lie. Often Satan uses the truth or half-truth to prove a lie or get someone to do wrong.

Satan said that Eve would know good from evil and "be as gods." Satan knew right from wrong, as did all the angels. In Job 1:6 and 2:1, the angels are called the sons of God. In the New Testament, followers of Christ are called "sons of God," John 1:12, Romans 8:14, Romans 8:19, Philippians 2:15 and 1 John 3:1-2. We are also "joint heirs with Christ," Romans 8:17.

No other creature on earth knows right from wrong. If you happen to come upon a grizzly bear with cubs, she couldn't care less who you are and it will not bother her conscience in the least if she rips and tears you into many pieces.

In 2 Timothy 3:1-4, it tells how people will be at the close of this age. In 1 Timothy 4:2, it also says that their conscience will be "seared by a hot iron." You see this today with all the murders and other crime. Even children kill their "friends" and have no remorse. Satan uses very subtle, elusive, delicate and indirect ways to fool us, just as he did with our first parents. The analogy is like the frog in water where the temperature is turned up very slowly until the frog dies. The poor frog does not realize that the water is getting too hot, because it is so gradual. Our society today is the same. The Lord knew that this would happen, that is why He warned us in the books of Timothy.

Apostle Paul had much to say about the "war in the flesh" that Christians must fight. In Romans 7:15, Paul speaks about the flesh causing him to do things he hates. In verse 17, he says that it is not he that does the wrong, but sin that lives in him. Then in verse 20, he says that because he does not want to sin, then it is not he that does wrong, but sin that lives in him. He goes on to explain in Romans: 8, that once Christ came and died and gave us the Holy Spirit, then we will have a spiritual mind and will not "walk after the flesh". Romans 8:5, "For they that are after the flesh mind the things of the flesh, but they that are after the Spirit the things of the Spirit."

Paul was hard to understand and even the Apostle Peter said so. What I understand from what Paul is talking about, is that once we have the Holy Spirit, it transforms our mind, and the Spirit and our mind become one. Our thoughts and intentions are molded together and this is the real you. Then, when we die, the flesh turns back to dust, but God's Spirit imprinted with our mind, our thoughts and memories is what lives on. Then, when we are resurrected, as was Christ, the "new man" will live forever.

This brings to mind what the Lord said in Leviticus 20:7 "Be ye holy for I am holy." 1 Peter 1:15 and 16, also repeats this and tells us to be holy. All holy means is "to be set apart". God said Himself that there are none like Him. When He swears, He swears by Himself. Jeremiah 12:16 and 22:5, are examples of God swearing by His own name.

This next part is difficult to understand and explain. When it first came to me, I had to ponder it a long time. When Satan was first created, he was good, but then iniquity was found in him. Ezekiel 28:15, "You (Satan, formerly Lucifer) was perfect in all your ways from the day that you were created, until iniquity was found in you."

I don't know if God *had* to create evil in order to separate Himself from it, but once iniquity was there, God had to set Himself apart from it. It could be like darkness. We would not know darkness if there was no light. God says that there is a mystery about the coming of iniquity or sin into His universe.

Just as God sets Himself apart from anything wicked, He expects us to do the same. He says in Isaiah 5:20, "Woe to them that call evil good and good evil." This is what is happening today. In the days of Noah evil and wickedness was everywhere and violence filled the earth, Genesis 6:5. Christ said, "As the days of Noah were, so also shall the coming of the Son of man be," Matthew 24:27.

Very little is mentioned about Christ when He was growing up, but there is one prophecy about Him as a young child. Isaiah 7:16 says that the young Christ will not know good from evil at first, but when He is still a child He will come to know and will "refuse the evil and choose the good." Therefore, this shows that as we grow up, we come to a point where we know good from evil. God has put this knowledge in our mind. Many choose not to follow it, however. The Bible says, "The wicked go astray from the womb," Psalms 58:3.

Chapter 28

What are the Seven Spirits of God?

In Revelation 3:1, 4:5 and 5:6, it mentions the "seven Spirits of God". Most know and understand of the "Father, Son and Holy Spirit, but what are the others. The Bible does not make it very clear. I searched and found many spirits mentioned, which could be some of the other "Spirits of God". Most ministers quote Isaiah 11:2 as listing the seven Spirits of God and this may be true so I will list them
First is the "Spirit of the Lord."
Second is the "Spirit of Wisdom."
Third is the "Spirit of Understanding."
Fourth is the Spirit of Counsel."
Fifth is the "Spirit of Might."
Sixth is the "Spirit of Knowledge."
Seventh is the "Spirit of the Fear of the Lord."
Isaiah 11:2 says, "And the Spirit of the Lord shall rest upon him, the Spirit of Wisdom and Understanding, the Spirit of Counsel and Might, the Spirit of Knowledge and the Fear of the Lord."
This is the way it is written in the Isaiah 11:2, but to me it does not make it clear that there are seven here. The Spirit of "Wisdom and Understanding sound like one to me, as does the Spirit of Counsel and Might. The Fear of the Lord does not sound like one of the seven Spirits, it sounds like it is wisdom. "The *fear of the Lord* is the beginning of wisdom, Proverbs, 9:10.
I feel the first one mentioned in Isaiah 11:2 the "Spirit of God" is definitely one of the seven. The "Spirit of

Wisdom" is also mentioned in other places in the Bible. The others sound like they could be and maybe they are, but I wanted to show what I found in the Bible during my research.

I found the "Spirit of Jealousy" in the Bible three times. God says several times that He is a jealous God and in Exodus 34:14, he said my name is *Jealous*. The first commandment is that "You shall have no other gods before me." The next commandment is like the first, "You shall not worship any graven image." The third says, "You shall not take the Lord your God's name in vain." This shows that the first three commandments are given so His people put Him first and give Him their love and respect. The other commandments are for man's relationship with others. God is jealous just as a husband is for his wife. God compares His "church" or people as a "woman", a "bride", or wife. A man becomes jealous if his wife flirts with another man or gives another man attention that he should be getting. God created man in His likeness and jealousy is one thing that man and God have in common.

The "Spirit of Truth" is mentioned in John 16: 13. Christ had a lot to say about truth and said that He bore witness of the truth.

The Spirit of Wisdom is mentioned four times so I am sure this is one of the seven Spirits.

I am not sure if all of these are counted as some of the seven Spirits of God. I have always wondered what the seven were and maybe we will not know for sure until the Lord returns. Here are seven I found in searching the Scriptures. Some of them may or may not be some of the seven but they are worth looking at:

First is the "Spirit of God." Countless times in the Bible and often called the "Spirit of the Lord."

Second is the "Holy Spirit." All through the Bible.

Third is the "Spirit of Christ." (The Word made flesh) Romans 8:9 and 1 Peter 1:11.

Fourth is the "Spirit of Truth." John 14:17, John 15:25, John 16:13 and 1 John 4:6.

Fifth is the "Spirit of Wisdom." Exodus 28:3, Deuteronomy 34:9, Isaiah 11:2 and Ephesians 1:17.

Sixth is the "Spirit of Knowledge." Isaiah 11:2

Seventh is "Spirit of Jealousy." Numbers 5:14 (twice) and Numbers 5:30.

If God's number for completeness is seven, therefore there are probably other things in His universe that are made up of sevens. Most likely, there are seven dimensions.

Chapter 29

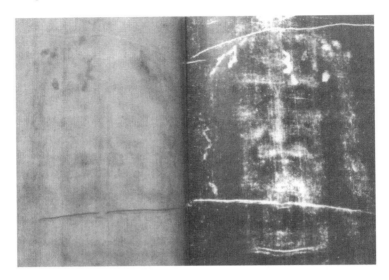

Is the Shroud of Turin Christ's Burial Cloth?

This is one of those questions where most believers in Christ think it is His actual burial cloth, while most non-believers think it isn't. This would be true even if it were proved to be genuine.

Some that don't believe have tried to "duplicate" the image on cloth with varying amounts of success.

The shroud of Turin is a linen cloth a little over fourteen-feet long and three-feet-seven-inches wide. Since 1578, it has been kept in a chapel of the cathedral in Turin, Italy. Before that, it was in the possession of a royal family of Italy and before that, a French nobleman had it. Before this, no one is certain. The Shroud closely resembles an artist copy of the Mandylion, which was a cloth taken to Constantinople in 944. If this is the same cloth, it was in

Urfa, Turkey in the 500's, but there is no history of it before this.

This large linen cloth was wrapped over and under a human body and on this very old Shroud, there is a very faint image of a man. The image is a total body image with the front and back visible. The image is so faint, however, that it cannot be seen up close, but if you step back several feet, the image becomes visible. The image of the man on the cloth is naked and dead. It is clear that it was a man who has been beaten, tortured and whipped by a whip with about 120 scourge marks. Not just any whip, but one like the ancient Romans used two-thousand years ago. His hands and feet have been pierced. His cheeks show that he was struck several times because they are swollen; one more than the other. His nose is crooked, but not broken. It also shows that he has many puncture wounds on his head, in a circle, as if by a crown of thorns. On his right side, between the fifth and sixth ribs, is a large puncture wound where he has been pieced by a sharp object like the tip of a sword. Forensic scientists that have examined the image have concluded the man that is depicted on the cloth was nailed where the wrist joins the hands (not the palms of the hands as most pictures of Christ show). His feet have large pierce wounds, too. The blood flow patterns are perfect from someone that has died by crucifixion. It has also been proven that the blood on the Shroud is human blood and that it was there before the image was made.

In 1898, the first photograph was taken of the shroud. To the shock and surprise of the photographer, the photonegative had a positive image on it and the positive image was a negative one! I myself have taken photos of the image from a book and the image on the negative and positives are reversed. It is truly amazing.

Probably the most startling occurrence happened when an image on the Shroud was put under a VP8 Analyzer Imaging Device that was used during the Voyager Project.

187

When it was viewed, it was discovered that *the image is three-dimensional* and with minute detail! Under this device, even the bones in the hands can be seen.

There was a terrific television program on the History Channel around 2012 called "The Real Face of Jesus" This program should be seen by anyone that is interested in the shroud. During the program, the people that worked with the shroud explained some fascinating facts. The image on the shroud "is a coded blueprint for *resurrecting* his image." The image is "not a painting". It is not a photograph but it is a "two-dimensional image with three-dimensional data encoded in it." The cloth was wrapped around a human body and the image was put on the surface of the cloth by "light" that was "scanned" onto it as a photo scanner/copier does today!

Tests were done several years ago (1988) by carbon dating and the results said that the shroud was only a few hundred years old (the late 1200's or early 1300's). Others point out that the cloth used for this test was taken along the border of the shroud where newer cloth was sewn to replace the damage caused by a fire during this same time period. Also, this part of the Shroud has been handled many times, which could give false readings of its age.

Recently, another cloth was discovered. It is a much smaller cloth (about the size of a small bath towel). It is called the Sudarium of Oviedo and it has documentation that it was in Spain about the year 619. The bloodstains on this cloth match perfectly the stains on the face of the shroud. Like the stains on the Shroud, this, too, has been proven to be human blood. A face cloth or "napkin" was commonly used to cover the face of the dead in the Middle East, especially by the Jews. In the Gospel of John 11:44 when Christ raised Lazarus from the dead, Lazarus had a napkin of cloth wrapped around his head. In John 20:7, it says that when Peter and John ran to the place where Christ's body had been laid, they found a napkin lying by itself and not with "the linen cloth" that He had also been wrapped in.

Pollen was found on the Shroud and face cloth and an Israeli botanist discovered that there were three types of pollen embedded in the cloth, which could only be found with a few miles of Jerusalem. One type of the pollen discovered came from a thorn bush that only grows within fifty miles of Jerusalem! Christ was crowned with a crown of thorns and this would have left pollen spores on His head that would have been transferred to the cloths. One other expert said that the linen cloth of the shroud has a "very distinctive weave." It is called a "3-to-1 herringbone pattern weave." This weave of the cloth is the same type of weave that was used in the first century in and around Jerusalem and a sample was discovered at Masada.

In my mind, there is more than enough proof that the shroud of Turin is the real burial cloth of the Lord. Of course, you will have to come to your own conclusion. Much of the reason many people do not believe that this is the actual burial cloth that coved Christ, is because it would prove that He did indeed rise from the dead. If they believed this, then they must also believe what He said. Christ said He was the Son of God and that He was coming back. He said many things and among them was that "But I say to you that every idle word that men shall speak they shall give account thereof in the Day of Judgment," Matthew 12:36. He also said in Numbers, 32:36, "…be sure your sins will find you out. Many more Scriptures show that God will hold people accountable for what they have done in this life. In Luke 12: Christ says, "For there is nothing covered that shall not be revealed, neither hid that shall not be known." Therefore, if the unbeliever accepts that Christ is who He said He was then they will have to stand before Him and give an account of what they have said and done. They do not want to face this truth; therefore, they do not *want* to believe. It will not matter, however, whether they believe or

189

not, for it will happen. "It is a fearful thing to fall into the hands of the living God," Hebrews 10:31.

I have also been told that there is a Jewish tradition that says if an innocent person was killed violently, that on Judgment Day the victim will show his murders the bloody clothes as evidence of their crime. This might very well be why the Scripture is in Revelation 19:13, "And He was clothed with a vesture dipped in blood, and His name is called The Word of God."

When the disciples were gathered one night after the Lord's resurrection, the Lord suddenly appeared in the room. This is in John 20:26-29. The Lord's follower, Thomas, had been told about the Lord's resurrection and how He had appeared before the other disciples, but he refused to believe. He said, "Unless I see the prints of the nails in His hands, can put my hand in the prints; unless I see the wound in His side and put my finger in His side, I will not believe."

This particular night Thomas was there and when he saw the Lord, he was shocked and stunned. The Lord then looked directly at him and said, "Reach forth your finger and examine my hands, and reach forth your hand and thrust it into my side and be not faithless but believing."

Thomas cried out, "My Lord and my God!"

The Lord then said, "Thomas you have seen and believed, but *blessed are those that have not seen and yet believe.*"

My opinion is that Christ left "His calling card". He left undeniable proof that not only was He here, but He was raised from the dead and is alive. This way all the "great minds" will have no excuse when He says, "I left positive proof that I was telling the truth, but you chose not to believe."

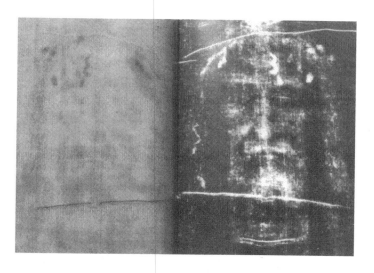

Above is the image I photographed from a book: The face on the shroud is encoded with 3D information. The left image is a positive, the right image, a negative. If you photograph it, the positive and negative will be reversed!

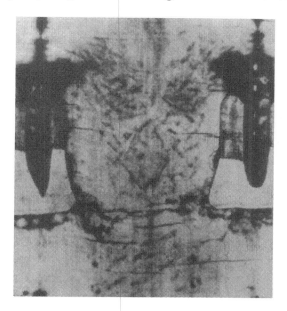

A negative photo of the image on the part of the cloth that was laid under the body. You can clearly see all the whip marks. "I gave my back to the smiters and my cheeks to them that that plucked off my hair. I hid not my face from shame and spitting," Isaiah 50:6.

Chapter 30

Prophesies in the Book of Psalms

Someone a while back posted on my Facebook page that there were "no prophecies in Psalms." I disagreed and gave a couple of examples that came to mind. I knew there were more so I took a look. Here are a few I found. Psalm 2:1-6 describes how the leaders of the world will try to destroy Christ at his return to earth. This is why the armies of the world go to Armageddon: "Why do the nations conspire and the peoples plot in vain? The kings of the earth take their stand and the rulers gather together against the Lord and against his Anointed One. 'Let us break their chains,' they say, 'and throw off their fetters.'

"The One enthroned in heaven laughs; the Lord scoffs at them. Then he rebukes them in his anger and terrifies them in his wrath, saying, 'I have installed my King on Zion, my holy hill.'"

Another, which is quoted by Apostle Paul in Acts 2:31, says in Psalm 16: 10, "For you will not leave me in the grave; neither will you let your Holy One (Christ) see decay". This is a prophecy about Christ's resurrection.

Psalm 17:15 is also about the resurrection of God's people, "I shall be satisfied when I awake with your likeness."

Psalm 22 is full of prophecies of the Lord's crucifixion. Psalm 22:1, "My God! My God! Why have you forsaken me!" is what Christ said on the cross at his darkest moment.

Psalm 22:16, "They pierced my hands and my feet." This was written hundreds of years before the Roman

Empire even existed, let alone used crucifixion as capital punishment!

Psalm 22:18, "They part my garments among them and cast lots upon my vesture." The Roman soldiers gambled for the Lord's robe.

As the Lord died, he said," Into your hands I commit my spirit," this is a quote from Psalm 31:5.

Psalm 39:9, "I was dumb, I opened not my mouth," is the same as Isaiah 53:7, "He was oppressed, and he was afflicted, *yet he opened not his mouth*: he is brought as a lamb to the slaughter, and as a sheep before her shearers *is dumb, so he opened not his mouth.*

In Psalm 40:7, it gives a prophecy about Christ's ministry, "Then I said, 'Lo, I come in the volume of the book it is written of me."

Psalm 41:9 tells of the betrayal of Judas. "Yes, my own familiar friend in whom I trusted, which did eat of my bread has lifted up his heal against me."

"God has gone up with a shout, the Lord with the sound of a trumpet," Psalm 47:5. This is the same as 1 Thessalonians 4:16, "For the Lord himself shall descend from heaven with a shout, with the voice of the archangel, and with the trump of God: and the dead in Christ shall rise first." This is a prophecy about the resurrection at Christ second coming. Psalm 50:3-4 is also about the Lord's return and the resurrection.

When the Lord returns, there will be the greatest earthquake that has ever struck the earth since man has been on it, Revelation 6:14, 16:18 & 20, Isaiah 24:19-20 and Ezekiel 38:20. It says in Isiah 24:19-20 that the "earth will wobble like a drunken man." In the other verses, it says every island will be moved out of its place and every mountain will fall. Psalm 60:2 says, "You have made the earth to tremble. You have broken it; heal the breaches thereof for it is shaken." The "breaches" are the cracks after the movements of the tectonic plates.

In Psalm 68:17, it speaks of Christ's return to resurrect his people and set up his Kingdom on earth. He comes from heaven and this prophecy tells us how he is coming, "The chariots of God are twenty thousand, even thousands upon thousands; the *Lord is among them*, (as in) Sinai, in the sanctuary." This clearly shows us how he will gather his people and then go to Jerusalem. If he comes from heaven, which is across outer space, then the "chariots" must be some type of spacecraft or perhaps different kinds of space ships. Some would have to be enormous to hold all the millions of people in the first resurrection.

Verse 22 from the same Psalm says that God's people "will be brought from the depths of the sea". "And the sea gave up the dead which were in it," Revelation 20:13.

Psalm 69:21 says, "They gave me gall for my food and they gave me vinegar to drink." This was why Christ said, "I thirst" as he was on the cross John 19:28-30, "After this, Yeshua knowing that all things were now accomplished, that the *scripture might be fulfilled*, said, 'I thirst'. Now there was set a vessel full of vinegar: and they filled a sponge with vinegar, and put it upon hyssop, and put it to his mouth. When Yeshua therefore had received the vinegar, he said, 'It is finished', and he bowed his head, and died".

The only place this prophecy was recorded was in Psalms. Therefore, this clearly shows that Psalms has prophecies and is not just David's writing glorifying God or giving thanks.

In Psalm 78:2 it again says, "I will open my mouth in a parable; I will speak dark sayings of old."

Psalm 79 tells of the future destruction of the Temple in Jerusalem and the murder of God's saints during the Great Tribulation at the end of time. It also says that God will "pour out his wrath upon the kingdoms of the earth verse 6.

In Psalm 82, it again talks about the earth being broken after the great earthquake and says, "All the foundations of the earth are out of course."

The next Psalm gives a prophecy that is right out of our newspapers today. Recently Iran's leader said, "We want to wipe Israel off the face of the earth!" Psalm 83:3-4, "With cunning they conspire against your people. They plot against those you cherish. "Come," they say, "let us destroy them as a nation, [so] that the name of Israel [will] be remembered no more."

Here is the scripture Satan quoted to Christ when he was trying to tempt him. Satan knew that Christ was protected during his life on earth so Satan tested him by telling him to jump from a high place at the Temple so people would know he was the Son of God. Satan knew what Psalm 91:11 and 12 said and said this to Christ, "For he shall give his angels charge over you to keep you safe in all your ways. They shall bear you up in their hands, lest your dash your foot against a stone."

Psalm 96:13 is a prophecy about the Lords' second coming and him judging the world as is Psalm 98:9.

Psalm 97 is a dramatic prophecy about the Lord coming in glory and power to earth at his second coming. In Psalm 102:13 and 16 speaks about the Lord "appearing in his glory"

The last one I will mention is a prophecy about how Christ would be rejected by the religious leaders of his people. Psalm 118:22, "The stone that the builders refused has become the head corner stone."

Here is even more positive proof that there are prophecies in Psalms because the Bible says in Acts 2:29-31, "Men and brethren, let me speak freely to you of the patriarch David, that he is both dead and buried, and his tomb is with us to this day. Therefore, *being a prophet*, and knowing that God had sworn with an oath to him that of the fruit of his body, according to the flesh, He would raise up the Christ to sit on his throne, he, foreseeing this, spoke concerning the resurrection of the Christ..."

There are many other prophecies in Psalms, so no; it is not just a book of praise but of predictions because David, who was a prophet, wrote them. Many of the prophecies have already come to pass. The other prophecies will likewise come to pass and with perfect precision.

Chapter 31

The "Lost Proverbs"

These are a few of the "proverbs" that I wrote long ago. I wrote many, but I wanted to leave you with some I really like: More are in my book, "The Book of WISDOM" (Words Instructing Spiritual Direction Of Man).

1: "The gift of God is life; the gift of life is God."
2: "One without a goal in life can only watch the game being played."
3: "Often a man does not count all that he has until has nothing to count."
4: "There is no end to the height or breadth or depth of heaven, yet God is there."
5: "Love does not see the filth that covers a man, but hate sees the smallest speck on his garment."
6: "A broken promise cuts deeper than a knife."
7: "The bigger a man's heart, the more room he has for God."
8: "Tears of joy will drown out the tears of sadness."
9: "If a man knew all the trouble that lay ahead, he would never leave the womb."
10: "A good word can change a life; a good life can change the world."
11: "There is no end to the wisdom of a fool."
12: "A poor man's knowledge is worth far less than a rich man's ignorance."
13: "A lie covers a thing, but love bears all."
14: "Don't relive the past, least you destroy the future."

15: "A person with ears prone to listen to gossip has lips prone to retelling it."

16: "A wife, who listens to her husband, loves God; a man who listens to God, loves his wife."

17: "A child knows all things, until trouble comes upon him."

18: "The self-righteous knows everyone's heart, except their own."

19: "What you don't want usually comes to pass; what you do, usually don't."

20: "You're a good friend when someone wants something from you; when you are in need, you are a stranger!"

20: "The easiest way is sometimes the longest."

21: "Often, the more people you meet, the less you want to."

22: "If money was as hard to spend as it is to earn, you would never run out of it."

23: "When friends are most needed, most are not friends."

24: "If a fool is born, a fool will die."

25: "If wisdom fell like rain, a fool would cover his head."

26: "The earth is but a grain of sand on the beach where God walks."

Chapter 32

Who was this Man called Yeshua?

This next part "Who was this man called Yeshua?" I wrote many years ago. I heard a preacher recite something like it and I thought it was good. I could not remember most of what he said, so I looked through the Bible myself and found Him in each book of the Bible. I'm sure that I could go back through the Bible and find many more things He is.

In Psalms 40:7 and Hebrews 10:7 it says, **"Then I said, 'I, lo, I come in the volume of the book that is written of me.'"**

He was born two thousand years ago in a tiny town in the Middle East. He never traveled more than thirty miles in any one direction. He was not special looking for He could easily blend into a crowd as He did on several occasions. Yet this one man has changed the world more than any other person in history.

He was born into a Jewish family and had the Hebrew name of Yeshua, which means "Salvation." He had no formal education. He was the first-born and growing up He worked with His earthly father as a carpenter. He also had several brothers and sisters.

So why was He so different from any other man that has ever lived? We must go to the Holy Bible to find out.

In the book of **Genesis**: He's the Creator, the Tree of Life, Noah's Ark and Abraham's Promise.

In **Exodus**: He's the Staff of Moses, the Manna from heaven and the Rock that brought
forth water.

In **Leviticus**: He's the Ten Commandments and the Holy Anointing Oil.

In **Numbers**: He's the Lawgiver and the Guide of Israel in the wilderness.

In **Deuteronomy**: He's the Giver of the Promised Land.

In **Joshua**: He's the Trumpet that brought down the walls of Jericho.

In **Judges**: He's Samson's strength.

In **Ruth**: He's the Root of David.

In **Samuel**: He's the Stone in David's sling that slew the giant.

In **Kings**: He's Solomon's wisdom.

In **Chronicles**: He's David's battle winner and Solomon's glory.

In **Ezra**: He's the Rebuilder of the temple.

In **Nehemiah**: He's the Watchman of the wall.

In **Esther**: He's the Sword of the Jews.

In **Job**: He's Job's Redeemer.

In **Psalms**: He's the Protector and Deliverer.

In **Proverbs**: He's Wisdom and Knowledge.

In **Ecclesiastes**: He's a Judge.

In the **Song of Solomon**: He's the Rose of Sharon and the Lily of the Valley.

In **Isaiah**: He's the Cornerstone, the Lamb of God, the Promised One and the Messiah.

In **Jeremiah**: He's the Branch of Righteousness.

In **Lamentations**: He's the Hope of Jerusalem.

In **Ezekiel**: He's the Breath of Life and the One with the fiery chariots.

In **Daniel**: He's the Man that shut the lion's mouths and the Fourth Man in the
fiery furnace.

In **Hosea**: He's the Punisher of Israel.

In **Joel**: He's the Strength of Israel and the Baptizer with the Holy Spirit and fire!

Yes, who was this man?

Well, in **Amos**: He's the Planter of His people.

In **Obadiah**: He's the Deliverance of His people.

In **Jonah**: He's Nineveh's Salvation.

In **Micah**: He's the Glory of Zion.

In **Nahum**: He is Revenger.

In **Habakkuk**: He's the Holy One.

In **Zephaniah**: He's the Restorer.

In **Haggai**: He's the Glory of the Latter House.

In **Zechariah**: He's the Redemption of His people.

In **Malachi**: He's the Refiner's Fire, the Purifier and the One to Come.

Now in the New Testament:

In **Matthew**: He's the Bright and Morning Star, a Babe in a manger, a carpenter's Son
   and the Cornerstone that was rejected.

In **Mark**: He's a teacher, a healer and a fisher of men.

In **Luke**: He's a man upon a donkey, the Bread of Life and a feeder of five thousand.

In **John**: He's the Good Shepherd, the Man dying upon a cross, the Way, the Truth,
   the Life and the Resurrection.

In **Acts**: He's the Light from heaven.

In **Romans**: He's the Love of God and the Salvation of the gentiles.

In **Corinthians**: He's the Foundation of Faith.

In **Galatians**: He's the Freedom of the curse of the Law.

In **Ephesians**: He's the Girdle of Truth, the Breastplate of Righteousness, the Shoes of
   the Gospel, the Shield of Faith, the Helmet of Salvation and the Sword of the
   Spirit. He is the Whole Armor of God.

In **Philippians**: He's Savior.

In **Colossians**: He's the Peace of God.

In **Thessalonians**: He's the Strength of the Church.

In **Timothy**: He's the Seed of David and the Holy Spirit that dwells within us.

In **Titus**: He's the Hope of Eternal Life.

In **Philemon**: He's Grace, Peace and Joy.

In **Hebrews**: He's the High Priest, the New Covenant and the Way of Faith.

In **James**: He's the Giver of Wisdom.

In **Peter**: He's the Chief Shepherd and the Giver of Crowns.

In **John** 1, 2 and 3: He's the Love of the Father and the Preserver of the Christians.

In **Jude**: He's the Executor of Judgment.

And in **Revelation**: He is Alpha and Omega, the Beginning and Ending, The Prince of Peace, the Everlasting Father, the Man upon the throne, the Lamb that's worthy, the One that sits upon a white horse and comes in the clouds with power and great glory, the One called Faithful and True. He is King of Kings and Lord of Lords. **He is God Almighty!**

Chapter 33

I Am Alpha and Omega

The First and the Last or I Am A to Z

Always keep me in your heart, your minds and your life
Believe in me and Believe all things are possible.

Count all your blessings.

Deceive not yourselves or others and Drink the Living Waters.

Entertain me in your thoughts and in Everything you do.

Follow your Messiah, for from the foundation of the world I have had a plan to save you.

God's hand, His love, His mercy and Goodness sustains you.

Hear my words and Hearken to them.

I Am the Lord thy God.

Judge not that you be not judged and always follow Justice.

Keep my Commandments.

Learn my ways, not man's.

Minister unto my children.

Never give in to temptation and have No other Gods before me.

Opportunity will always be present to witness for me if you Open your heart.

Promises I make will never be broken.

Question man's doctrines, but Quench not the Holy Spirit.

Rejoice and **R**emember your **R**edemption draws near.
Seek me and the Truth, both of which are the same.
Turn from your own ways and **T**rust in Me.
Understand my ways.
Vengeance is mine, but **V**ictory is yours.
Waste not the life that I have given you.
X is a cross where I redeemed you.
You are mine and I gave myself for **Y**ou.
Zealous I am for my own.

Christ's Name spelled out

What's in a Name?

Below is an excerpt from my book "Beyond the Grave: Is there life after death?" I have mentioned some of this before, but this excerpt has more in it.

I wanted to reveal a truth that many do not know. If you have seen the Mel Gibson movie, "The Passion of the Christ", you may have heard Christ being called by His Hebrew name of Yeshua. This was the name He was given at birth. In the first translations of the King James Bible, His name was Iesus because the J was not yet used. Those that translated the Bible into English, thought the name Yeshua was not masculine enough. Therefore, the *h* was taken out and the *a* was dropped at the end and an *s* replaced it. They then replaced the Y with a J, which spells Jesus.

Many names in the Bible have been changed when it was translated into English and other languages. Since the J was not used in biblical times, Jerusalem began with a Y as did Jacob, James, John and so forth. Other names, too, have been changed. Even Joshua is a translation of Yeshua. The Y was changed to a J at the beginning and the e changed to an o.

The most important name, however, is our savior's name. "Neither is there salvation in any other: for ***there is no other name under heaven given among men, whereby we must be saved***," Acts 4:12.

Yeshua means "Salvation." Any time you see salvation in the Bible you can replace it with Christ's name of Yeshua. By doing so it often gives a much deeper meaning to the scriptures and shows that He was and is all through the Old Testament long before He was born as a human. The first time that salvation is used is in Genesis 49:18, "I have waited for your "Salvation" O Lord."

This scripture comes alive and speaks volumes when it reads, "I have waited for your Yeshua O Lord." There are 164 times that the word "salvation" is used.

Here are a few scriptures with His name in place of "salvation." This is only a few. Job 13:16, "He also *shall be* my Yeshua: for a hypocrite shall not come before him."

Psalms 18:46, "The LORD lives; and blessed *be* my rock; and let the God of my Yeshua be exalted."

Psalms 38:22, "Make haste to help me, O Lord my Yeshua."

Psalms 68:20, "*He that is* our God *is* the God of Yeshua; and unto GOD the Lord *belong* the issues from death," (the resurrection).

Psalms149:4, "For the LORD takes pleasure in his people: he will beautify the meek with Yeshua."

Isaiah 12:3, "Therefore with joy shall you draw water out of the wells of Yeshua." Remember what Christ said to the woman at the well when he told her He would give her water and she would never thirst again? John 4:10-11, "Christ answered and said to her, 'If you knew the gift of God, and who is the *One* saying to you, 'Give Me to drink', you would have asked Him, and He would give you *living water*. The woman said to Him, 'Sir, you have no vessel, and the well is deep. From where then do you have living water?

"The *one* believing into Me, as the scripture said, 'Out of his belly will flow rivers of living water.'" In John 7:38,

This shows clearly that Isaiah 12:3 was a prophecy of Christ coming to give eternal life to those that believes.

Isaiah 56:1, "Keep justice and do righteousness, for My Yeshua *is* near to come, and My righteousness to be revealed."

Isaiah 62:11, "Behold, the Lord has made *it* to be heard to the end of the earth. *Tell the daughter of Zion,* **Behold! Your Yeshua comes!** Behold! His reward *is* with Him, and His work before Him."

These scriptures say much more when you understand that Christ's name is "Salvation."

You already know that Yeshua means "Salvation" but here is one more mystery of the Bible that is astounding. Each letter in the Hebrew alphabet also stands for a letter, and the letters in His name says it all!

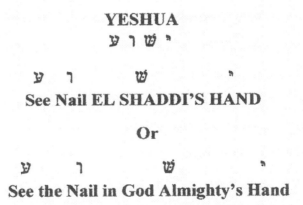

YESHUA

ע ו שׁ י

ע ו   שׁ   י

See Nail EL SHADDI'S HAND

Or

ע ו   שׁ   י

See the Nail in God Almighty's Hand

How awesome is that! Yes, Yeshua means **salvation,** and anytime you read in the Bible the word *salvation* you can put His name in that sentence and the Bible shows you even more how He saves us. Therefore, in this book, I will use the name Yeshua instead of Jesus.

What about God the Father's name? God's name consists of four consonants (a Tetragrammaton), usually YHWH or YHVH. No one is certain how it is pronounced because the vowel sounds had to be added by those pronouncing it. In biblical days, only the High Priest knew how to say God's name and they kept the pronunciation secret, believing his name was too sacred to be spoken aloud. Therefore, they would not tell anyone how to say it because they were afraid if someone knew how to say His name, they might use it in vain and thus sin. God, however, wants His name published. "But I have raised you up for this very purpose, that I might show you my power and that *my name might be proclaimed in all the earth*. Exodus 9:16-17.

Most know his name as Yahweh, but in all other words in Hebrew, there is no W sound. In fact, the V came before the W and the W is just two VV's placed side by side. Most likely, the name would be spelled Yahveh. This is how my brother writes it and pronounces it, as do many Messianic believers. Some shorten the name and just say Yah. It is certainly not Jehovah because the J was not used even in the English language until the mid-1600's. God is also called Elohim (Hebrew for God) and El Shaddai (Hebrew for God Almighty).

Christ, called God our Heavenly Father. Christ was also called I Am before He came in a human body.

About the Author

Kenneth Edward Barnes has been called, *"A modern day Mark Twain"* by a local newspaper reporter. *"He shows a Twain sense of humor in conversation and in his writing. He writes in the 'down to earth' style that Twain used to capture the heart of America."*

He was born on April 4, 1951, along the banks of Little Pigeon Creek in the southern tip of Indiana, downstream from where Abraham Lincoln grew up. As a child, he loved fishing from the muddy banks of the creek and roaming in the nearby woods. He never missed an opportunity to be in the outdoors where he could see all of God's creation.

Ken is a nationally published writer, poet and the author of over one hundred books. Some of his most popular ones are: *The Mammoth Slayers; A Cabin in the Woods;*

Mysteries of the Bible; Madam President; Life Along Little Pigeon Creek; A Children's Story Collection; The Golden Sparrow; Buddy and Rambo: The Orphaned Raccoons; Outdoor Adventures; The Arkansas River Monster collection, and Do Pets go to Heaven? This could soon change, however, as he has recently written several others.

The author became a member of *Hoosier Outdoor Writers* in 1993, where he has won several awards from them in their annual writing contest. He has also been a guest speaker for the *Boy Scouts, Daughters of the American Revolution, Teachers Reading Counsel, Kiwanis Club*, and at several schools, libraries and churches.

Ken has been an outdoor columnist and contributing editor for several newspapers and magazines: *Ohio Valley Sportsman, Kentucky Woods and Waters, Southern Indiana Outdoors, Fur-Fish-Game, Wild Outdoor World, Mid-West Outdoors,* and a hard cover book titled *From the Field.* He has written for the *Boonville Standard, Perry County News, Newburgh Register and Chandler Post.* He has had poems published locally and nationally. One titled *The Stranger* went to missionaries around the world. The poem, *Princess,* was also published locally and nationally, and won honorable mention in a national contest. His best-loved poem is *Condemned* and has been published by the tens of thousands. Nearly every single poem he has written is in his colored paperback book, *Poems from the Heart* and *My Favorite Poems.*

Ken has worked for an Evansville, Indiana, television station where he had outdoor news segments aired that he wrote, directed and edited. He also had film clips that were aired on the national television shows *Real TV* and *Animal Planet.* At this time, he has several short videos on YouTube and on GodTube.

211

Studying nature since childhood, he is a self-taught ornithologist and a conservationist. In 2009, he became founder and president of the *Golden Sparrow Nature Society*, the name of which was chosen because of his first published book. Ken loves to share his knowledge and love of nature, and it has been said that he is a walking encyclopedia on birds and animals. Because of this, he recently published an e-book titled *Birds and Animals of Southern Indiana*. It has over 300 photos of birds and animals, most of which he photographed himself. He frequently updates it with new photos.

He has followed his dream of being a writer since 1978 and now lives in a cabin in the woods. Being an individualist, he cleared the land, dug a well by hand and built the house himself, which uses only solar electric. He even wrote a book titled *Solar Electric: How does that work?*

Comments or questions on the author's work can be left on his Facebook page at: **Kenneth Edward Barnes**, or on **Twitter** at **Kenneth Edward Barne @BarneKenneth.** All of Ken's books can be seen on his **Author Page** at Amazon.

Books by Kenneth Edward Barnes in:
Paperback, Hardcover and E-book

1. In Search of a Golden Sparrow
2. Life on Pigeon Creek
3. Barnestorming the Outdoors
4. Invasion of the Dregs
5. A Children's Story Collection
6. Poems from the Heart
7. The B.O.O.K. (Bible Of Observational Knowledge)
Under the pen name of ZTW

Books available as E-books only:

1. Is There a Devil? Is Satan Real?
2. The Thirteenth Disciple
3. The Two Witnesses
4. The Mammoth Slayers: Why the series was written
5. Birds and Animals of Southern Indiana
6. The Ancient Art of Falconry
7. Solar Electric: How does that work?
8. The Book of WISDOM (Words Instructing Spiritual Direction Of Man)

9. Instruction Manual for the WIFE (Wonderful Idea From Eden)
10. How to Care for your MAN (Mate's Animalistic Needs)
11. How to Raise your CHILD (Cute Huggable Innocent Little Darling)
12. INSTINCTS (Interesting Nature Secret Tendencies If Nature Could Teach Secrets)
13. The Adventures of Ralph and Fred
14. Twelve Tantalizing Tongue Twisting Tales
15. The Last Mammoth
16. A Squirrel Named Rufus
17. Pete: The Poor Pig
18. The Bike Ride
19. The Great Yankeetown Easter Egg Hunt
20. King and Tippy: Two Special Puppies
21. The Wanderer of Little Pigeon Creek
22. The Panther
23. A Legend Comes Alive
24. The Eagle and the Hummingbird
25. The Grumbling Grasshopper
26. Buzz: The Cowfly
27. The Watermelon Turtle
28. I Don't want to be a Pig!
29. Who? What? When? Where? Why?
30. Buggies: (Also, includes: Animal Cracks and other jokes and riddles)

Available as Paperback and E-books:

1. A Biblical Mystery: Christians need to become a Jew: What does this mean?
2. A Cabin in the Woods
3. A Day Appointed
4. A House Divided: This is why Donald Trump won the election
5. A Rude Awakening
6. Abortion: Why all the controversy?

43. The Arkansas River Monster: The complete series
44. The Black Widow
45. The Book of HUMOR
46. The Capture of the Arkansas River Monster
47. The Coming Invasion
48. The Creature of O'Minee
49. The Day that Time Stood Still
50. The Five Dimensions of Sex
51. The Golden Sparrow
52. The Last Arkansas River Monster
53. The Long Pond Road
54. The Invasion of the Dregs
55. The Mammoth Slayers
56. The Mammoth Slayers: Last Clan of Neanderthals
57. The Mammoth Slayers: The Last Neanderthal
58. The Mammoth Slayers: The Prequel
59. The Mammoth Slayers: The Trilogy
60. The Ruby Ring and the Impossible Dream
61. The Unexplained
62. The War on Christians
63. The Words and Life of Jesus
64. Thou Shall Not Kill: What does God think about the killing of animals?
65. To Keep a Secret
66. What in the World is Wrong?
67. Why Does God Let Bad Things Happen?
68. Words to Live By

Printed in Great Britain
by Amazon